MENTAL TOUGHNESS

Improve Your Self-Confidence and Develop a Positive Mindset.

Train Your Mind to Achieve Success by Following These Healthy Habits.

Henry J. Jenkins

Table of Contents

Have you expected your satisfaction to come from other people's approval? Look in the mirror.

Introduction

I used to know a man who thought that success happened because of luck; he always proved his point with the fact that the world wealthiest people today are not more hardworking than the poor, and as a matter of fact, poor people do more hard work and challenging jobs than the rich. Yet, the rich keep amassing wealth, while the poor keep getting poorer.

The reality of the first paragraph is seen in every area of the world, and today, I choose to tell you that you can only be successful if you have the right attitude towards success. Do many poor men have the right attitude towards success? How many defeated people have the right mindset to approach the fear, or failure, or defeat? People often deduce success to luck simply because they do not believe they can be successful in life. Besides their mindset, people who associate success with luck are also people who practice unhealthy habits.

In my few years as a professional, author, and coach, I have realized that mental toughness is the collective result of every habit, activity, and reaction that you engage in. Think of the last time you failed at a particular task, the next time you attempted that same task, and it became easier for you. The truth is experienced in life teaches us to become resilient. I have had my fair share in life; I have had to deal with bad friends, failures, loss of a job, contracts, financial droughts, and bad relationships. I have dealt with life in different areas, but every time I look back at such times, I remember how better I have become. I see the growth and development that has happened in my life.

Mental toughness is not independent of failure, habits, mistakes, and our environment. We become better by engaging in different activities around our immediate environment. Moreover, mental toughness occurs when you have great and healthy habits. I wrote this book when I realized that habits are critical in our lives. I have certain habits such as maintaining eye contact while talking to someone, reading from news journals daily, not skipping family time amid others. I have realized that my health, success, and relationships can only be fruitful with healthy habits. Hence, I wrote you this book to help you get better in life.

This book contains 33 rich chapters. Each chapter deals with different titles ranging from habits, environment, fear of failure and fear of success, proactive and positive thinking, mistakes, and many more. I will implore that you read this book with an open mind, and trust me; you will benefit a lot from the book.

May I welcome you to this life-changing journey?

Chapter 1: Fear of Failure

The fear of failure is many times internal; fear is a facade that makes the possible impossible. Have you ever had to make some pivotal decisions to your success you could not because you were scared of failing? Have you ever rejected some amazing offers and opportunities from potential helpers and bosses because you were uncertain about your results? Perhaps you had your mind fixated on how bad you would do rather than how great you would be. I have learned over time in life that failure is a normal phenomenon; failure makes us stronger. Failure leads to faith, and having faith in oneself produces resilience. Amazingly, every successful person out there has their share of failure. However, the big question is, should you fear failures? Should you live every day of your life feeling scared that you would fail at college, at your job, or in your marriage? No, you shouldn't do any of that.

The fear of failure produces lethargy, weakness, and a negative mindset. Being scared to fail means you are anticipating failure. Here is a scenario:

Jack Williams is a business analyst, a first-class graduate from the University of Exeter, where he bagged a degree in Business and Management. Jack had always lived in the shadow of himself throughout college; despite his good grades, he believed he would not make a good business consultant as he has always imagined. Due to his good grades, he always got referrals and recommendations for job opportunities; however, he always flopped during the interview. He was always nervous and anxious; hence, he either goes blank when asked some basic questions or leaves the interview session before it ends.

This pathetic journey lasted for six months; Jack had no job, while his friends with lower grades had well-paying jobs. He was frustrated about his problem, and this made him sought help from a thought leader. During the coaching process, Jack was asked his greatest fear and his greatest motivation. He answered, *"My greatest fear is failing and making mistakes in my career."* The thought leader nodded her head and gave him a smile to answer the next question.

Jack said, *"I am not sure I have a great motivation; however, my fear motivates me. The reason I studied Business Management is that I want to be a business owner. But, I am scared I would fail as a business owner if I don't study this course."* Jack paused, stared at the thought leader, and continued his statement, carefully choosing his words because he had never reflected on such questions all his life.

"I don't know why I feel scared. I lived with the fear that I would never get a good-paying job all through college if I get anything lesser than a first-class. Now, I have a first-class degree, yet, I am scared I will not be able to fit into these positions and deliver my work promptly because I am uncertain about my abilities." Jack sighed. It was apparent he had said all that was a burden to him. His thought leader smiled at him again and asked him to take a deep breath in and out.

Here is what his thought leader said:

Failure is normal. At various points in our lives, we tend to experience failure, but the fear of failure will only cripple your ambitions and aspirations. When you occupy your mind with your failures, weakness, and mistakes that you are yet to make, you tell your mind that you are not good enough to make some moves. Moreover, the fear of failure is internal and mental; the mindset gradually wears you off and gives you the idea that your dreams are invalid and your goals are challenging to achieve. I will like to make a few references to Jack, and I believe you saw that Jack stated that he has always lived in fear; his good grades were not achieved from a place of self-confidence, but rather from a place of fear of failure.

Choosing the fear of failure as a motivation is a bad motivation; rather than producing a good result, it leads to bad outcomes. Think of the last time you passed exams because of fear; many times, you lack the confidence to defend your results. I believe that Jack lacked self-confidence in his grades and himself. He had always lived in the delusion of himself, hence accepting the reality that he would be a great Business Analyst was difficult. Need I say this, your responsibility as an individual is to believe in yourself and your abilities. Don't be like Jack; it is okay to make mistakes, but never dwell on it. Make a move, and when you fall, rise again. The journey is a long haul, and you need a strong mental capacity to keep moving.

Are you like Jack? Do you struggle to make decisions without the fear of failure, distracting, or distorting your mind? Here are 5 points to overcome the fear of failure.

Define Your Fear

Jack was asked to define his fears, and he realized what his fears were. Right now, I want you to answer the question, "what is your greatest fear?" It is the fear of failure; for some, it is the fear of divorce and stigmatization. But, regardless of your fear, you need to define it and write it down in your journal.

Shine the Light of Positivity on Your Fear

Fear travails amid the darkness. Fear triumphs more when you take it more personally and gives it power; hence it begins to control your life. After defining your fear, shine the light of positivity on your fear. If you have always believed you cannot be a successful doctor, begin to affirm that you will be a successful doctor. However, you need to take steps that would drastically reduce fear in your mind.

For example, suppose you have always believed you will not be a successful nurse because you have difficulty understanding anatomy and physiology. In that case, you need to take some steps towards understanding anatomy better.

Reframe Your Goals

What are your goals? What do you want to become? What are your aspirations and ambitions? It is important that you reframe your goals and perhaps start small. If you're going to be the next most successful digital strategist in this century, ensure that you break your goals down into shorter goals.

First and foremost, create a three-month goal; for instance, show up on your social media page every day, create value, and help people for 60 days. After this, you can organize a webinar for people. Having a big goal is not bad if you have all the resources and the ability to achieve them; it is not a problem. However, you should break your goals into short-term and long-term goals.

Prepare for the Unknown

Many people find it challenging to overcome the fear of failure because they have overtime drowned in the impossibility mindset. They have believed they cannot achieve anything in life, and thus they have struggled to make the right choices. One of the ways to overcome failure fears to prepare for the unknown. What are the possible things that may occur when you are making a new decision? Need I say that preparing for the unknown is not the same thing as dwelling on failures or impossibility. Prepare for the worse, yet have your mind fixed on the goal. I have learned that individuals who never prepare for the unknown find it difficult to get over negative situations around them.

Speak Positive Words to Yourself

The fear of failure is internal, and if it must be combatted, it should be dealt with internally. I encourage you to have your personalized list of daily affirmations that you must speak to yourself. You can create your affirmations, or better still, here are some affirmations to help you build a positive mindset:

- *I am healthy and confident*

- *I am successful*

- *I dare to achieve my goals and take risks*

- *I am not weighed down by my insecurities and the impossibilities that surrounds me*

- *I believe in my abilities, my self, and in my strength*

The fear of failing is the genesis of failure itself. Avoid failure like the plague. Wake up every day with the mind of a winner. You can achieve it. Your dreams are not too big, and they are valid.

Chapter 2: Fear of Success

Success is beautiful. However, success is not an event. Many people assume that success has a particular sound, look, or color. No, that is entirely wrong. Success is just success. While many people have their definition of success, we cannot but say that success is relative. My definition of success may be quite different from what you define as success; nonetheless, the fear of success is everywhere.

Do you struggle to embrace leadership positions? Do you hate to lead a team for whatever reason? Do you find it difficult to accept responsibilities and accountabilities? Do you feel bad or shy when you are being praised for your hard work? If yes, then there is a tendency that you have a fear of success. Whenever I want to make a new decision at some point in my life, I fright at the thought of making new plans, taking risks, and making new choices. I used to struggle to embrace the truth about my leadership skills. I was scared of being a leader, facing the crowd, telling people what to do, and being responsible for others. But, when I realized that the growth I wanted would never occur if I kept growing at such a pace, I changed my mindset, and success became mine.

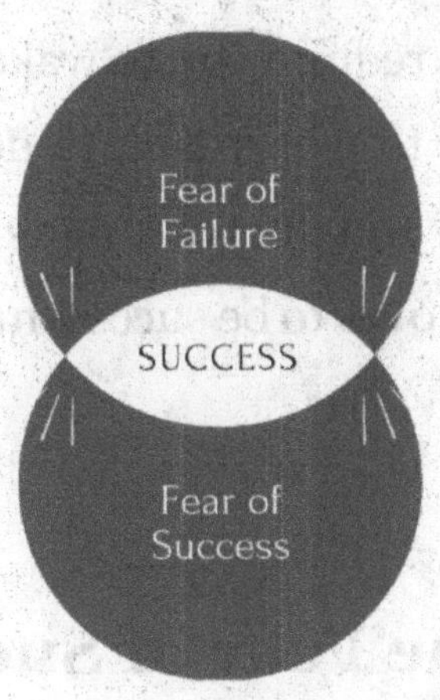

The fear of success can be subtle as procrastinating a major project, turning down great opportunities under the disguise of stress, and lack of resources. Many times, when I see a young person turn down great opportunities, I ask what is stopping them and holding them back. Sometimes, it is not fair, and it is just the fear of success. Whenever you are procrastinating on a big project, such as not sending the proposals for a business project, not collaborating for an event or campaign, not submitting your resume for a job, and many more, then you may simply be scared of success. Brain Tracy said, "We are our worst enemy," and I cannot but agree more. Why do you think you stop paying attention to activities that will help you get better or stronger? It is because success is difficult to achieve than failure.

Achieving success needs a lot of exercises, plans, and actions. You need to be both committed and responsible for your life and actions to become successful. However, it is different from failure; failure does not require you to wake up at 4 am every day to study before getting to work. Failure does not ask you to be committed to your plan and purpose, and only success does that. And I believe everyone loves to be successful, why then are people still scared of success?

What Causes the Fear of Success?

The fear of success can be relative to different individuals. According to Psychology Today, people who have experienced trauma in time past may easily associate their excitement of success with the reactions they experience due to traumatic experiences. Due to this reaction, these individuals often avoid excitement or unusual emotions that accompany successful situations, which creates a phobic and myopic mindset about success.

On the other hand, many people fear success because they have, over time, created what success should look like in their hearts. Like I mentioned earlier that success has no specific definition or color. Many people, especially young people, have conditioned their minds to think that success only comes after suffering, losses, or several failures. As much as this may be true, success is relative to different individuals. Bill Gates did not lose his job or start fending for himself at the age of 13, Brain Tracy had his share of failure, but his story is different from Mark Zuckerberg's. The truth is failures are inevitable; however, not everyone loses all they have before becoming successful. If you have the mindset that you have to get sacked from your workplace, lose your job, lose your goods, run bankrupt, get jailed over debts, then your mind has been wrongly programmed. It is time you ensured that you begin to walk out of the negative mindset and conditions you have given yourself. Not every successful person lost all that they have, and you do not necessarily have to lose all that you have to become successful.

Anxiety is also another causative agent of fear of success. Many people are anxious about how they would act when they are rich, famous, and successful. Some people are nervous about how to go about their leadership positions. If you feel this way, take a deep breath whenever you feel that way, and ensure that you speak something positive.

How to Overcome the Fear of Success

Track the Origin of the Feeling

Many people who live with the fear of failure are embarrassed to talk about it. Hence, it is tough to help them out. While some individuals do not know they are living with the fear of success. You must understand how you feel. Identify the cause of fear. The moment you acknowledge the cause of fear, then you can overcome it. To track the origin of this fear, you may need to start journaling. Here is the process of journaling:

1. Start by writing whatever drops in your mind whenever you think of the fear of success

2. Have you ever felt that way before? Write down the feeling and what triggered the feeling.

3. Find the best way to avoid such a feeling next time or work around the feeling.

Here is a scenario:

If you have always struggled to complete a massive project, then find out what triggers the feeling of fear whenever you attempt to complete the project. When next you have such a feeling about your incomplete project, get on the job, and tell yourself you will complete the job.

Stop Avoiding Strategies and Activities That Will Make You Successful

After uncovering and tracking the origin of fear, begin to embrace the activities and strategies that will help you become successful. Activities such as completing a project, submitting your resume, submitting a business proposal, attending an interview should be embraced. Moreover, when you stop avoiding strategies and activities, you begin to eliminate the fear of success. You intentionally teach your brain to embrace success, which reduces the fear of success.

Get Professional Help from a Psychological Therapist

Having a fear of success can be difficult because it can hinder you from getting many things and achieving many things. You must understand that it is good to try and understand the source of your fear. However, you may not understand this fear on your own; hence, you need a professional's help. A mental health coach can be of value to you. Moreover, studies have shown us that most people who fear failure have one time or the other experienced traumatic experiences. Another reason you need to visit a therapist is that people who fear failure suffer from anxiety disorders.

Affirm That You Are a Success Already

Affirmations are great ways to boost your confidence, become better, and reflect on who you are. Many individuals, both young and old, struggle with the fear of success because the struggle is real. Affirmations will be of great help in overcoming the fear of failure. Here are a few affirmations that you must confess daily:

- I am a success already

- Whatever project I lay my hands upon shall succeed

- I experience financial prosperity and physical prosperity at all times

- My business and life flourish on all sides

In summary, endeavor to validate the source of your fear of failure, face your fears, seek professional help, and help yourself by affirming positive things alone to yourself. The fear of success may be a big mountain for you, but it can be made low if you follow the steps mentioned above.

Chapter 3: Are We The Result Of Our Environment Or Can We Create It?

We are products of the world we live in. Likewise, the world has become what we made it. Today, there are over 7 billion existing globally, and every one of us has our differences. These differences are due to the environmental factor and background that most people have. The truth is people act based on their background and environmental factors. Environmental factors greatly impact an individual's total well-being in all forms; the medical, spiritual, mental, and physical aspects. Truly, we are the results of our environment, but we can create our results. We can ensure that we don't look exactly like our background and environment, and we must know that we can create a new world, the world we desire and want.

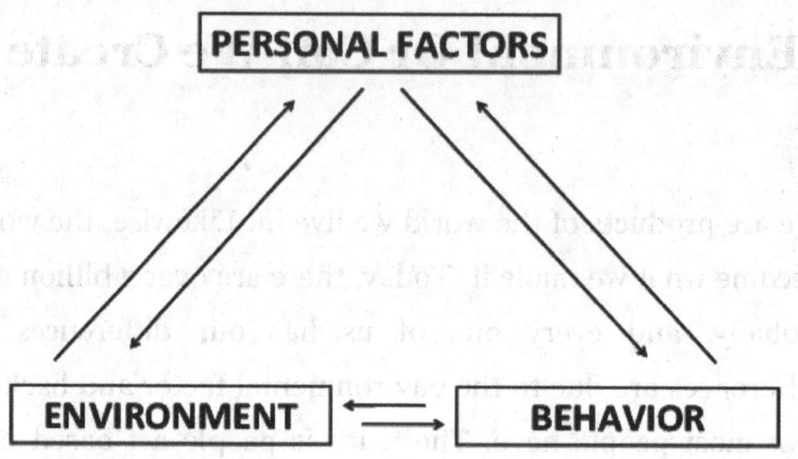

The year 2020 brought many changes to the human race; the year started with nations wars, proceeded to the rise of the global pandemic, and amid this global crisis, the globe stood still when a police officer killed certain black Americans. One of the things I observed during all of these events was that we could change our environment. We have the power to build the world that we desire to live in. Each time I check today, I see new trends and new hashtags, and these elements have been overtime used as a tool of change in the world. It is time you believed that you could change the world even from your corner. It is high time you realized that no input is too small, and no effort is wasted. If you wonder why this chapter's title is made in this form, you may need to have a little reflection on things around you. You need to ask

28

how your environment influences you and the various impact on our behavioral patterns.

How Our Environment Influences Us

The human mind interacts with the environment in diverse ways. The moment a child is born, the child begins to grow. As the child grows, he hears different words from different people; the child eats what others eat and says what others say. As the child grows, the environment's effect becomes more evident in the child's life. The child begins to look like the rest of the people in society and may also be at risk of various diseases that affect other people in the family. Here are three ways our environment affects us:

1. The environment can affect the behavior of people and also influence the way they act. For instance, a child born in a slum has more tendency to abuse drugs, is involved in illegal acts more than a child raised in a more conducive and healthy environment. The environment can also impact a man's thought process, such that an individual may have a certain thinking pattern different from his other counterparts. For instance, an Indian individual may think differently from an American because of their national and ethnic background.

2. Our environment influences interactions between people. One of the reasons you can find it easy to communicate with some people in your environment is because you both share the same environment, and you both have the same environmental background.

3. Our environment can affect our mood. For example, in the pandemic's heat, many people were recorded to suffer depression, and pandemic inclined mood swings, because of the fear attached to the pandemic. Likewise, when certain unfortunate situations began to happen in the latter part of the year 2020, many people were scared and afraid. Moreover, our immediate environment, such as our room and offices, can also affect our mood. Previous studies stated that rooms that contain bright light, whether natural or artificial, could improve mood and health outcomes. Besides, a lighted room can improve sleep, reduce depression, anxiety, and agitation.

What are those things you have always wanted to change in your environment or background? What are the things you have struggled to manage in your background? Do you know that you can change all of these things? You can become a world changer, a peacemaker, and an influencer. The truth is change begins with you.

How to Change Your Environment

Changing your environment or creating a new environment can be difficult; I have seen this countless times in our various spheres of lives. I have realized that creating a new environment can be a major challenge, especially when the changes involve other people's lives. It is even worse if the demanded change is religious or political. You can make some changes in your life, and in the life of others, as long as it is for good, but I must remind you that it can be a war between you and the rest of the world. I think creating a new environment can be called revolution.

I believe that it is better to change your environment rather than patch things up or renovate things. Certain things are wrong in your workplace, family, or the immediate environment; I have realized that it is better to create a new world by scarping the things that are not working rather than renovating the things that are not working. Moreover, this chapter is focused on changing your immediate world and not the whole world. Changing the whole world or your nation can demand you to pay a lot of sacrifices, create enmity for you, and make you feel lost in the world. Am I saying that you should not aspire to be a global changer? Well, I am not saying such. Instead, this chapter focuses on becoming a change agent in your family and amidst your friends. The truth remains that there are certain things that you must change in your life if you want to be successful. On this note, one of the major skills you need before creating a new environment is to make your decisions right. Decision making is very critical, and you cannot change your world without first thinking about it. Here are examples of things you must put into consideration before making any decision:

- What are wrong or ills happening in your life or around you?

- Prioritize the negative situations around you that need a change. For example, do you struggle with narcissist bosses? Do you have trouble with your relationship? Do you find it difficult to ace your exams? Do you think it is difficult to be a successful businesswoman? Imagine that the above-listed struggles are yours, then how would you prioritize it. Which of the following will be placing more priority on?

- Take note of the various events that may unfold if you create a new world for yourself. Take note of the number of friends that you may lose. Think of the negative impact of your decision on your life.

Many people do not want to change their world because they are unwilling to make some life-changing decisions. Some people are not willing to let go of friends, lose jobs, and relocate. I have realized that you must be tough-minded if you want to be a world changer. You should never be disturbed about what others think about you; it may look insane to others around you, but trust me, you will get better and succeed.

Moreover, changing your environment makes it easy for you to do what is right because the right and healthy environment contain enough motivation. If you organize your environment enough and clear away every doubt and hurdles on your path, achieving success can be much easier, and you can have enough reason to practice better habits. Many times, many people think that creating a new environment should be internal. That is, it should start from within. But I believe that change can occur anywhere, whether internally or externally. You may need to change yourself first if the subject of change has to do with belief, mindset, or religion. However, if you already have the right attitude, you need to change those around you by living by example, discussing the importance of change in others' lives. I want you to optimize changing your environment by lending your voice when you hear people say wrong things or do wrong things. The truth is the little things we do can make a large impact on our lives and our society. No doubt, changes may not occur immediately. The changes may occur little by little, but the goal is to remain a change maker.

Chapter 4: Habits as Implanting Ideas In The Subconscious

Every human has habits that they perform every day; activities like sleeping, eating, exercising, reading, listening to music, and many more activities. Habits can be defined as small decisions that you make and series of activities you perform daily. According to Duke University research, habits are responsible for at least 40% of our behaviors at any given time. The truth remains that you are a result of your habits and activities.

I can boldly say that your life is essentially the sum of every habit that you practice daily. Your success can be determined by the number of good habits you practice day in and day out. What are those activities you involve in every day of your life? How long do you spend reading books every day? Whatever you do, every day has the power to change you, whether positively or negatively. Moreover, past studies have stated that practicing the same habit for at least 21 days tends to become a habit. At the same time, Brian Tracy stated that practicing the same job for six years tends to make you a Guru in that field.

I believe that habits are like drops of water. I think you must be familiar with the statement little drops of water make the ocean. Hence, little practice of activities makes it become a habit. For instance, you are a writer; one of the habits may include writing every day. Certain writers have their specific routine per day, and some people write 300 words daily, some 500 words, while some 2000 words. Depending on your level of expertise, or the need for development, every writer is expected to write every day. As a writer writes daily, he builds a wealth of knowledge and increases his capacity to acquire new information.

Healthy habits have a way of infusing the right knowledge into our subconscious. For instance, if your daily habit includes reading for the first 4 hours of the day, you will realize that you would begin to find yourself having the desire to read after practicing it for few days. Habits can implant several ideas in our minds in different ways, and that is why you need to invest in inhabits.

Why You Should Invest in Healthy Habits

Research says that 40% of your actions are most times conscious. However, your habits are big parts of your life that you may not notice. It simply means that there are certain habits that you may exhibit without you knowing you do them. Yes, habits are essential elements in our lives, and you must invest in them. The following are the reasons you need to invest in healthy habits:

Your Life Is the Total of Your Habits, Whether They Are Positive or Negative

I have realized that when successful people are asked about their success story or their activities daily, quite a number of them mention their habits. I once stumbled on the richest men's sleeping routine globally, and I realized that most of them practice, such as sleeping for at least 6 hours every day, going to the gym, reading, and eating fruits. These exercises and activities did not make Bill Gates a wealthy man, and rather it enhanced their capacity to make wealth easily.

Your Habits Allow You to Take Control of Your Life

If you have a specific sleeping pattern and daily routine, which has turned out to be a habit, you will observe that you can easily take control of your life by doing so. In the previous chapter, we looked into changing your world; however, you can not successfully change your world if you have not cultivated good habits over time.

For instance, if you want to reach your firm's apex position, you will need to be proactive, make the right decisions, have high integrity, and be loyal. However, integrity is not a habit; certain people are referred to have high integrity because they have overtime showed actions worthy of emulation. But, habits like not telling a lie, being truthful, be accountable with responsibilities can prove your integrity before others.

On the other hand, habits allow you to take control of your life. I want you to reflect on the last time you wanted to make some decisions, and your habits came into play.

Habits Never Disappear; Instead, They Are Overpowered by Other Habits

Many people assume that they outgrow bad habits, but the truth remains that you cannot outgrow bad habits. Other habits can only overpower them. If you have always lied as a young child, and you stopped lying in your teenagehood. You should never say that you have outgrown lying, or the reason why you stopped lying is that you are now older. Having that mindset is disastrous and would only make you see habits differently. Whether you have bad or good habits, they can remain a part of you for a very long while. Often, we exhibit the habits needed for a specific place, which is why there are high possibilities that you will change your habits when you switch job, career, workplace, or home.

Chapter 5: Types of Habits

As a young individual, I used to think that having a healthy daily routine was unnecessary, and I often felt they were ineffective. I have always thought that habits do not do so much more for us than our actions, but I realized that our habits fuel our actions. Simply say that our actions are the result of our habits. When I discovered that my habits would affect my life and productivity, I began to pay attention to my habits and actions. In my discovery course, I learned that there are majorly two habits: bad and good habits.

What Are Good and Bad Habits?

There are majorly two types of habits, good and bad habits. I believe that everyone has good and bad habits, and these habits can be exhibited in different forms. However, it is your duty as an individual to discern between good and bad habits. Examples of good habits include sleeping early, eating healthy, working out daily, spending time with your family, and reading. Simultaneously, bad habits include arguing, not sleeping properly, not eating well, finding it difficult to settle the dispute and disagreement with others keeping malice, and not exercising. Every habit tends to impact your life and career. An individual who does not eat properly tends to be malnourished or obese, and diseases may begin to set in. I will encourage you to write down the habits that you have, both good and bad habits. After writing all of these habits, pay attention to the bad habits you must work on, habits you must change and improve:

Do you have a list of daily habits? I have a list of habits that I must practice daily, and I believe many people do. Although I have realized that most people who are successful have a list of habits they practice daily. Here are examples from the world richest and most influential people:

- Bill Gates, the founder of Microsoft, a billionaire, and philanthropist, spends at least an hour on the treadmill, watching courses from the Teaching Company.

- Barack Obama has his morning workout and cardio exercises at 6:45 am, before having breakfast with his family. Barack Obama called himself a night owl in an interview. He gets to the office at around 9 am, works till 6:30 pm, and then spends time with his children. He reads new papers or any other form of reading before going to bed at 12:30 am.

- Donald Trump wakes up every day or 5:30 am and starts making calls by 6 am. He spends the remaining hours in the morning reading and tweeting before starting his day at 11 am. Although Donald Trump is the President of the United States, each day varies. However, he doesn't eat breakfast; neither does he take coffee to wake. The report says that Trump sleeps for 3- 4 hours at night.

- Billionaire Warren Buffet spends hours of his day reading over 70 pages of a book daily. His daily goal is to ensure that he returns to bed smarter than he woke up. Warren Buffet starts reading early morning before going for his daily business.

- Oprah Winfrey, the successful entertainment billionaire, has a more detailed morning routine than most billionaires. She spends some hours on the treadmill, after which she meditates before having her breakfast, which is always a nutritious breakfast.

It is evident that successful people today have daily habits that they practice, and over time these practices have improved their lives and productivity.

Types of Habits

In my life and work, I have observed that there are three categories of habits, which are namely:

Personal

Every successful person has a list of personal habits that they practice, which may not be peculiar to the general public. For example, Donald Trump does not believe that he should sleep for more than 4 hours every day. He believes that every successful person should not sleep for more than that. In contrast, Mark Zuckerberg wears the same shirt every day. Mark wears the same shirt daily, and he wakes up at 8 am on the dot. While some other people may disagree with the idea of wearing the same clothes every day, for different personal reasons, Mark chose to wear the same shirt every day.

One of the secrets to personal habits is that these habits have to be practiced daily and consistently. Moreover, most personal habits are unique to the individual. I have learned from experiences that many young people do not understand that many personal habits are unique, and you do not need to imitate their habits. Imitating habits makes you unreal and makes you lack creativity. I have heard of some people who try to imitate the daily routine of successful people around them, and sometimes, these imitation does not lead to a positive result. Does this mean that you should not imitate others? No, I never meant that. Instead, it would help if you first understood why such an individual has such a personal habit before jumping into following them.

Having understood this, you must ensure that your practice habits are related to your goals and life. For example, Stephen King, who happens to be one of the most successful living writers in the world today, writes every day. He starts writing between 8 am and 8:30 am, and he does not stop writing until any time between 11:30 pm and 1:30 pm. Other successful people in the world all have different habits, and another example is Lionel Messi. Messi said in an interview that he has many habits, and he prefers to leave his table ready for the next day.

Creating a personal habit is easy; all you need to do is create the list of habits you want to practice daily and consistently practice them. The goal is to get better. Hence, you must ensure that you create a routine. For example, you can start by creating a routine to read ten pages of a book daily. Consistently doing that will help you get better, and you subconsciously begin to read more books as the day goes by. Personal habits have high tendencies to imparting your everyday life. Ensure that you choose habits that are related to your goal.

Behavioral Habits

Behavior is referred to as the manner of life of an individual. An individual's behavior depicts the mannerism, pattern of life, and individual's gesture in simpler terms. Behavioral habits are simply habits that affect the manner and pattern of life of an individual. Many times, habits and behavior are used interchangeably; however, behavioral habits involve actions and activities that involve the individual's natural behavioral pattern. For instance, good behavior includes being respectful, keeping to words, staying up late at night, eating slowly or fast, talking at all times, and many more. These examples are behaviors because they are natural things that most individuals were not dedicated to keeping. For instance, some teenagers eat slowly, not because they desire to chew foods slowly, but because that's the way they have always eaten their foods.

Having understood the elements of behavior, behavioral habits entail natural ways of life that are turned into habits over time. For instance, I used to know a girl who ate slowly in high school because she always had a book in her hands because of the long minutes at the café. At first, I wondered why she loved to read, she was addicted to reading, but in one of the long conversations with her, she said she decided to spend her lunchtime reading a few pages of the book.

Other behavioral habits may include helping older people with their loads and luggage in any public place, making sure to clean the dishes after use, do laundry daily, and many more. On the other hand, behavioral habits can vary from both good and bad. For instance, an individual may find it easy to disrespect others and keep malice with other people. The bottom line of behavioral habits is that they go a long way in helping you build a reputation before the people around you. If you don't have such good behavior, I will encourage you to change your behaviors and change your ways.

Credentials Habits

The credential can be referred to as a series of competence and qualifications that represent an individual. Credentials are commonly known as certificates, results, and many more files that show an individual's educational and professional level. Credential habits are a series of habits that put you on the edge of professional and academic success. Many times, people do not understand that there are diverse inhabits. Certain habits are specific for a professional environment, while some habits are healthy for your relationship. For instance, sending love notes is a healthy habit for a relationship and not for the workplace. Instead, habits such as communication and teamwork should be of much value to organizations and professionals. Credential habits for business owners and entrepreneurs include wake up early, set daily goals, pursue long-term goals, read business books daily, and many more.

Moreover, even in the business world, certain professionals have different and diverse credential habits. For instance, a doctor and nurse always has to be proactive, listen to people, and have healthy communication habits. For example, my herniated disc has been checked by doctors from different specialties. According to the osteopath, it was best treated with manipulations, the orthopedist said it was treatable with the torso, for the physiotherapist with massages, by the neurosurgeon with surgery. Taking for granted the good faith of each of them, the solution was seen within their world of knowledge. Each one gave the answer that his culture and technical-scientific and personal training allowed him; each of these professionals had, in their opinion, the cure for my healing – each one had their paradigms beyond which very little existed. Beyond just their credentials and expertise, each of these healthcare professionals had certain habits that made it possible for them to take care of me properly.

These three categories are essential, and they can be seen in almost every successful person's life. Every successful individual spends each day of their life developing new habits. The essence of having healthy habits is to remain productive and effective in business and life. Moreover, life is quite wide and tough, which is why you need to be resilient to achieve your goals. Like I always say, every wall is good to drive the carpenter's nail, but the question is, is the carpenter's nail stable and strong enough to bear the burden of whatever object the carpenter wants to place on it. Many people face different situations in life, and they tend to react based on the general view that others have about life. However, it is not done that way. You must select the best for you, find out the habits you need in your personal life, relationship, and career, and begin developing them. In summary, always remember that your success story boils down to how much you are willing to invest in yourself.

Chapter 6: Paradigms Imposed With Credential Habits

The Cage in Which You Live and Which You Even Paid for Without Realizing It

In the previous chapter, we examined various kinds of habits. We saw the good, the bad, the personal, behavioral, and credential habits. This chapter is dedicated to shedding more light on the credential habit by making us more aware of the various paradigms imposed on us. Further, it tells us how we can escape from being caged by such habits.

We have paid for so many things. Our loved ones or we bought much stuff we use in life. But have you ever thought or imagined that you could ever pay for a "cage" where you could be locked in without even realizing it? Isn't that a puzzle? It's that puzzle that I hope to unravel in this chapter.

What Are the Credential Habits?

You will agree with me that certain professions come along with certain habits, abilities, a peculiar set of thinking and skills, qualifications, and manner of talking, and even dressing mode.

These peculiarities, habits, and behaviors imposed on us by our careers or professions are referred to as credential habits. They are habits gotten as a result of our credentials or qualifications. They represent a series of competence, certifications, and qualifications that represent an individual and put them on the edge of professional and educational success.

In the business world, various professions have various credential habits. For instance, a nursery school teacher always has to be patient with the students, understand that each student doesn't assimilate at the same rate, be strict but tender, and have great storytelling skills because children love stories. For entrepreneurs, the habit of credentials might be to get up early, be self-motivated, set long-term objectives, read about trends in their industry, and many more. Also, note that the ability to understand which credential habit is suitable for a specific professional environment is an important skill.

Paradigms as Patterns of Thinking

I see paradigms as a kingdom of thought processes, ideas, or ways of cultivating philosophies. It's a system of thinking and doing things bounded by several peculiarities. Since change is paramount, no paradigm is meant to remain forever. Therefore a paradigm shift is a drastic departure from a given thought process, ideology, or philosophy.

It happens every time. Century by century, we see changes in systems, patterns, and methodologies. Technological advancements and innovative capacities often engender these usurping of former paradigms through thorough research and development.

Paradigms Imposed with Credential Habits

There are certain paradigms imposed on us by our credentials. You know you are under such a paradigm when all you can think, feel, do, has to be related to your profession. For instance, a medical doctor has been programmed to view all things from a medical perspective. If anything occurs right before a doctor, he thinks of medication and medical implications of any action.

A banker also has been programmed to view things from a monetary perspective. He thinks of counting and keeping other people's money. A teacher may believe that life is all about teaching others and even forget to be quiet and learn from others.

These and many more are the various paradigms that our professions impose on us without us even realizing it. Yes, specialization is good, but it might have you caged without your notice. If you only focus on one aspect of a particular field due to the need to specialize and ignore other things, and then a shift occurs that sweeps away the relevance of what you used to know, what would you do? You might be forced to ask the question – who moved my cheese? That's why some have advocated that while it is good to know everything about something (specialization), on the other hand, it is great to have an idea about everything (generalization).

How Credential Habits Make Us Caged Without Realizing It

Is it hilarious that one can be caged without his notice?

Here's a scenario:

Alexander's dream has always been a fashion designer, although he studied accounting and finance in the university. He always wanted to implement his skills and knowledge in the finance industry to build a very profitable fashion business.

However, when Alex was through with school, he was faced with a lack of capital to pursue his dream. Rather than staying idle, he decides to take up a management consulting firm role since he was qualified for it. He got the job and started working. Initially, he intended to stay in the job for a maximum of two years, but when he was narrating this story, he was already clocking nine years on the job. He has risen to the position of a senior manager.

Every year he gets to repeat the same line: "This year, I'll be done with this job," but before he realizes it, it's year-end, and another year is around the corner. Some of Alex's colleagues noticed that he had some flair for fashion as his looks were constantly top-notch. He always wore unique blazer jackets with perfect shoes and briefcases to match. While at his desk, his dream of becoming a fashion designer keeps hunting him. He doesn't feel satisfied or fulfilled. He feels like he's been trapped. That's how credential habits can have us caged.

Another story is Martin's. A senior colleague of mine while I was interning in an accounting firm. He has worked for about three to four years, but you could feel that he wasn't satisfied with his firm's role. Although he had his ICAN certificate and got the job, he wasn't fulfilled. His credential has caged him in that profession.

What can we do?

When we find ourselves in professions where we feel unfulfilled and caged, what do we do? Do we remain so and stay unhappy for the rest of our lives? Or do we take a quantum leap out into the unknown? Or do we begin to follow our passion as a side hustle while we keep the job?

I do not think there is an all-encompassing and straight forward answer to this question. I believe the answer is based on the individual. The bitter truth remains that not everyone is cut out to be an entrepreneur. Not everybody can manage start-ups and oversee the total organization of a company.

Some people are just so great at being complementary leaders. They are not the main bosses; they tend to lead better when they find themselves in the middle of the pack. John Maxwell calls them the 360-degree leaders. So these kinds of people may not do well if they go out on their own. What they can do is to determine what they want. It could be that they only want to have their start-up because everyone around them is chanting 'be an entrepreneur' and not that they have a passion for it. After a proper self-assessment, they might discover that they can succeed in the organization, rise to the top, and become prosperous. The idea of being an entrepreneur is actually for them to be entrepreneurial in their thinking. They could study how money works and make their money work for them through having a diversified portfolio of investments while they keep their job.

For those who want to take a quantum leap into the business, I suggest that they begin to do underground study, research, and ask questions about the line of businesses they are passionate about even as they work on their jobs.

As they do so, they could be saving money alongside. Or if they intend to take a loan, it's also cool. But I think their savings are better. I'm sure you don't want us to talk about the emotional strain that can follow borrowed money.

When they've saved up enough and learned what it takes to begin, they can quietly resign and kick off their practice. Some who have walked this path say that they love it because they control their own time. Another point to note is that this path requires you to be a self-directed person because you are now your boss.

And as for those who would love to follow their passion, they would rather make it the second option instead of their main career path; these people keep their jobs, and they are similar to the above category. They begin studying and even launch their passion alongside, and if it doesn't disrupt their schedule at work, they tend to juggle both or put someone in charge of it, and when it becomes fully blown to sustain itself, they can resign and attend to what they love.

I can imagine the feeling. Honestly, doing what you love makes you feel like a free and happy bird. In all, I think it's best if our credential habits and the profession we choose to pursue are actually in line with what gives us fulfillment. In that way, we won't have to struggle because we would be doing just fine.

Chapter 7: First Level (Basic) and Derived (Second Level) Habits

The behavior and patterns that you showcase by default are referred to as habits. They enable you to carry out vital activities like brushing your teeth, taking a shower, and preparing for work. Isn't it quite interesting that you follow this routine every day without considering it? Those habits you exhibit unconsciously create room for your brain to carry out more advanced activities like journaling, problem-solving, daily meditation, or choosing what book to read.

Someone has rightly said, "We are creatures of habits." This statement implies that your daily routine can determine if you will be a success or even a failure. Why? Because of your actions, both conscious and subconscious, stem from your habits. Your habits also determine your personal and professional productivity level, bringing us to the concepts of essential habits and derives habits.

What are the basic habits?

I also call these first-level habits. They could be personal and even behavioral. These habits ensure personal success or failure. They could as well be healthy or harmful.

Some examples of healthy basic and personal habits could include

- **Sleeping Early:** Depending on your schedule, it generally pays to sleep on time. Research has shown that an average adult requires about six to eight hours of sleep to function at peak performance. When you sleep on time, you tend to wake up early, plan your day, and get to work early. Sleeping early enables you to wake, and that enough makes you in charge of your day.

- **Eating Healthily:** Brian Tracy has rightly said that the key to a long healthy life is to eat less and exercise more. Avoiding junk and all sorts of sugary foods is another way to eat healthily. Eating lots of fruits and vegetables is also a vital, healthy habit.

- **Working out daily:** Exercising your muscles and bodies daily is one of the good habits to have. You do not necessarily have to start with some vigorous exercise like running a marathon or begin lifting heavyweights. All you need could be to simply engage in less strenuous activities that oxygenate your blood and stimulate the release of endorphins into your body. Jack Dorsey, the CEO of Twitter, also classified exercise as a good habit to maximize his very busy schedule. According to him, he wakes up by 5 am, meditates for thirty minutes, does a seven-minute workout three times, makes coffee, and then checks in. He once said on Product Hunt that he follows this routine daily because it keeps him steady-state, thereby empowering him to be more productive.

- **Spending time with your family:** According to Gary Chapman, one of the five love languages is "Quality time." Spending quality time with family is a basic habit that makes your relationships smooth and full of love. Research has shown that couples that don't spend quality time together tend to drift apart emotionally as there's no real bonding among them.

- **Reading:** Reading is a healthy basic habit that can generally improve the quality of anyone's life. It relaxes our minds, broadens our horizons, and stimulates our creativity. Benjamin Carson has one of my fact quotes on reading. He said, *"If we commit ourselves to read, and this increases our knowledge, only God can then limit our growth."*

Other basic personal habits could be unhealthy. For instance, habits like;

- **Engaging in constant arguments:** Most people can't go a single day without arguing. They just know how to steer every conversation to an argumentative front. They leave the main issue to be tackled and attack the individual engaging them in a conversation. It's unhealthy.

- **Eating unhealthily:** Unhealthy meal combination and eating so late at night are also examples of unhealthy eating habits common to most people. Eating unhealthily also entails having no regard for a balanced diet, taking junk food, and excessive sugar.

- **Keeping malice:** Due to envy and strife, which resides in the heart of some, keeping malice has become a habit for them. They hold grudges and cling unnecessarily to their feelings of hurt. Psychologically and emotionally, it's not healthy.

- **Overeating:** This has even become an addiction for some people. They eat anything they set their eyes on just to satisfy their craving for food. The problem with overeating is that it might lead to obesity.

- **Not sleeping correctly**: Refusal to get enough sleep can be harmful to your body and general productivity. Feelings of tiredness and drowsiness might be your lot throughout the day if you do not get enough sleep during your night time.

- **Refusing to exercise**: Most people fail to realize that exercise doesn't necessarily have to be cumbersome. Just a five-minute workout session daily can improve the quality of your life.

- **Procrastination:** Putting what you can do now to a later date. And usually, we end up not doing it because "the time is never always right." My suggestion to you is simple: JUST DO IT.

- **Smoking:** Not everyone has this habit, but it's basic to most people. It's generally unhealthy, and that's why boldly written on the pack is the statement "smokers are liable to die young."

What Are the Derived Habits?

I also call this second level habits. They are habits that are picked up along our path to personal and professional success. They could also be referred to as credentials habit because these habits also empower us for success in our careers and professions.

Here, an individual has to be deliberate about these habits because they are learned and consciously practiced to be fully maximized.

Consider some of the following second level habits:

Beginning Your Day with Meditation

I highly recommend mindful meditation practice early in the morning. Meditation promotes calmness of the mind, which helps you to stay in the present moment. It also enables you to be mindful of the challenging situations you face during the day. Several stressors may trigger as your day goes by, but meditation helps you maintain calmness before taking on the challenges. Personally, it helps me strategize and think about ideas. Meditation is a vital habit that I recommend to everyone because it helps connect with both the things in your life and your environment.

Managing Your Time

Another great habit is the act of managing your time effectively. It goes a long way to impact your achievement. A wise man once said, "If you love life, then don't squander time, because that's the stuff life is made of." Time management happens to be one key factor that differentiates between leaders, successful people, and others.

How to manage your time effectively? Let's consider Jack Dorsey's recommendation in one of the Technology events. According to him, He accomplishes effective time management by theming his days and practicing self-discipline. These themes help in handling distractions and interactions. Whenever he gets a request or a task that's not aligned with the day's theme, he doesn't do it.

His weekly theme is shown below:

- Mondays – Management

- Tuesdays – Product

- Wednesday – Marketing and growth

- Thursdays – Developers, and partnerships

- Fridays – Culture and recruiting

- Saturdays – Taking off

- Sundays – Reflection, feedback, strategy, and preparing for Monday.

As a result of such a time-effective management strategy, while others struggled with one job, he could successfully run two companies.

Setting Daily Goals with Intentions

Everyone has goals. Such goals may relate to personal or professional life. The truth is, we're all tending towards one direction or another. Nonetheless, while long-term goals can offer you direction and a long term perspective, it's your daily goals that you set that help sustain the momentum to keep moving toward your long term goals.

Now, here's the real truth: Successful people do not set goals without stating clearly their intentions. According to Jennifer Cohen of Forbes, *"What helps you achieve your desired expectation is ensuring that intentions accompany your daily goals."*

Seeking Inspiration

Of course, it is usually challenging to be inspired for quite an extended period.

Sometimes, we get discouraged and feel like giving up on our goals when things do not work out as we intended. A practical habit you can develop to stay on top of the situation is to inspire yourself each day. Get yourself motivated. How can you do that? You've meditated, you could watch some motivational videos and allow the story of great leaders to inspire you. Remember, inspiration is fuel for achieving greatness.

Following the Pareto Principle

This is another great habit for your professional success. 80/20 rule or Pareto's Principle simply means that twenty percent of the tasks yield eighty percent of the results in any given situation. So you can maximize your productivity by investing most of your energy, time, and resources on those specific tasks that will generate the most impact. Once you're done with those tasks, you shift your focus to other activities on your to-do list.

Learning to Do Things One at a Time

Asides from any other thing, it improves your concentration, and there is power in concentration. Some studies reveal that only two percent of people in the world can multitask successfully.

Although there's no harm in multitasking occasionally, constant juggling between tasks could limit your focus and lead to mental clutter.

Moreover, a study conducted by Stanford University also reveals that heavy multitasking could lower efficiency and may impair your cognitive control.

I have a story about this. I know a guy in high school who decided to study multiple books at the same time while he was preparing for exams. He would place three to four different subjects on his desk and keep reading each of them simultaneously. When results for that particular exam came out, his grades dropped. This was a guy who was usually on top of the class.

This is why you should form a habit of single-tasking as much as possible. You could make a list of things you need to accomplish on a particular day. Start with the most important and make your way down the list, ticking them off, one after another.

Mastering the Art of Listening

Effective communication is vital when it comes to personal and professional success. You will agree with me that listening is central to communication. Paying attention to what others have to say will make others feel loved and important and enable you to understand them better and have a fresh perspective. Learn to listen to what they have to say and what they mean by what they say. Non-verbal cues are important as well. The more you listen to good counsel, to great people, the more you will learn and increase knowledge.

Chapter 8: Positive Mindset to React With Personal Habits to the Paradigms Imposed by Credential Habits

One of my role models always said: *"The mind is the battlefield of every success."* The implication is that it's not the war without that really matters, but the war within. That war that goes on in our minds. This is so serious that no matter how many external forces want to push you to greatness, if your mind isn't comprehensive enough to accommodate such push, it will sabotage it, either consciously or unconsciously. When talking about habits, the need for a positive mindset cannot be overemphasized.

The mindset that tells of a person's pattern of thinking, belief system, and idiosyncrasies could either be positive or negative, and several factors are responsible. Maybe a person's experience or the system they were brought up in.

Positivity doesn't necessarily refer to simply smiling and being cheerful all the time. However, it tells of your overall perspective on life and your tendency to keep your focus on the good and great side of life, the setbacks notwithstanding.

It also speaks of the ability to see the opportunity that's right in the adversity.

What is a Positive Mindset?

You probably know what a positive mindset is already, but it will help us begin with a definition. According to Remez Sasson, *"Positive thinking is a mental attitude that focuses on the bright side of life and expects positive results."* Another definition we could consider as comprehensive is that of Kendra Cherry at Very Well Mind. It says:

"Positive thinking is defined as approaching life's issues with a positive outlook. It does not necessarily mean ignoring or avoiding bad things, or even pretending that bad things do not exist, but rather, positive thinking is about making the best out of every challenge, ensuring that you always look at the best in people, and believe the best of their abilities."

Extrapolating from these definitions, we can come up with a description of a positive mindset as the tendency to focus on the brighter side of life, expect positive outcomes, and approach challenges with optimism. Having a positive mindset entails making positive thinking a habit, continually searching for the opportunity within adversity, and learning to make the best of whatever situation you find yourself in.

A positive mindset is willing to drive the change required to better the lives of the individual involved. It's never fixed in a rut as it always seeks an opportunity to lead a better life.

There are several traits and characteristics associated with having a positive mindset. Some of them are:

Optimism

Optimism refers to the desire and willingness to make an effort and take a chance rather than assuming your efforts won't yield results. Many psychological tests have proven that happy people seem to have a uniqueness that allows them to enjoy life and live a more fulfilled life than an average person.

Surprisingly, this uniqueness is nothing more than optimism!

A piece of great news about optimism is that it can be learned, which means you can learn how to think differently and positively when you adopt an optimistic mind. In reality, if you say and do what other healthy, happy people with positive mindsets and attitudes say and do, you will soon feel the same way, get similar results, and enjoy similar experiences as they do.

Acceptance

This talks about acknowledging the fact that things won't always turn out the way you want them to, but you're humble enough to learn from your mistakes.

Resilience

When you're resilient, you easily bounce back from adversity, disappointment, and failure rather than giving up. I know a friend of mine whose apartment was gutted by fire. Rather than sitting down and mourning all her life away, she got over it within a day, moved in with another friend of hers, and continued her work with the little stuff she had outside the building. Within a short time, she raised money, got a new apartment, and lived happily there. She understood that just sitting and being sorrowful won't solve an inch of the ground.

Gratitude

There are great and amazing things in your life. Gratitude talks about actively and consistently appreciating the good things in your life.

Note that these traits are not just characteristics of a positive mindset, but they could also work in the other direction. That is, actively adopting optimism, acceptance, resilience, or gratitude in your life will help you develop a positive mindset. A positive mindset will also give you a positive attitude, and with a positive attitude, you can look adversity in the eye and laugh. You can look at the seemingly impossible situation and say: Yes, I can. You can use the power of a smile to reverse the tone of a situation. You can get back up if you fall. You can be a source of energy that lifts those around you. You can envision a positive future no matter how critical your current circumstances are, and very important, you can have the courage to be happy for someone else's success.

Paradigms Imposed by Credential Habits

There is a saying that 'change' is the only 'constant' in the universe. Most of the things we have in our world today were not here a few years ago. Some of the belief systems, cultural orientations, patterns of thinking, and doing things we have now were not here a few years ago.

The advancement in technology has revolutionized the entire space, and even certain careers path that we never thought of have emerged. For instance, if you told a person who lived in the 19th century that we would have something like the career of a social media manager or a digital marketer, they might think you're going nuts. Why? Because social media wasn't available at that time. But what do we have now? It has become the social media age. Conversations on social media have become so serious that Nations even communicate with their citizens via social media; successful campaigns for brands are held on social media.

The presence of a lockdown even amplified it the more, where individuals had to depend on the use of social space to reach out to one another since physical contact was restricted. Companies sought ways to work from home using several online platforms.

All these are what we can refer to as paradigm shifts – a shift in the pattern of thinking and manner of doing things.

Credential habits, which I also refer to as professional habits, the habits of your profession have also imposed on us certain paradigms. Several work processes aren't the same anymore. Let me give an example. In this day and time, you can't say you are a successful marketer if you do not have an idea of the digital space and leverage it for your marketing success.

While effective communication and teamwork are credential habits for an organization, you will agree that there is a different way to communicate in the digital space. If you desire the attention of people, there's a different way to communicate using social media.

How a Positive Mindset Can Influence Your Credential Habit

A positive mindset cuts across several areas of life. It can greatly influence the habits you exhibit. One quality of a positive mindset is flexibility. That is being flexible enough to see and believe that something good can come out of a particular situation. Being flexible enough to see that there are better levels and that your world view isn't going to be the best there is all the time.

When you have such a perspective, you will see the shift in paradigm as a good thing. You will see the need to learn the art of effective communication using the digital space. With a positive mental outlook, you will begin to see how this new pattern can be a force for good for your business or organization. You must be willing to adjust and to grow. You must be willing to change. A mentor of mine once said, whatever is not changing is not growing, and whatever is not growing is dying. In essence, a positive mindset is a strong force that keeps you going, motivated, and willing to keep adjusting to the shifts in paradigms we would always have in our world

Chapter 9: Get Out Of Your Box With The Success Paradigm

The impact of good habits on the life of individuals can never be overemphasized. As you grow older, especially in your 20's and 30's there is this constant reminder from people around, articles you read, and also all-around social media, the need to make the most of yourself, evolve, develop your talents, manage your time, live your best and most accomplished life and numerous other motivational guides that opens your mind daily to the need to keep pushing.

Unfortunately, when a person has not built his/her mind and set his/her daily routines with the discipline required to create that image, actualize that ambition and achieve those goals, these supposed motivations might turn around and channel the person into depression and a failure-mindset.

Creating success paradigms talks about models for getting yourself out of the box you already choked yourself in by credential habits. Forming new habits is centralized around a new redefined goal. For instance, the desire to be accepted by a person you admire physically might be the central goal that will wake you up to the establishment of some new habits, such as keeping to a healthy diet routine (both to shed weight and to be healthy), taking skincare routines seriously, reading books (even though you may only be getting books that are synonymous with the title "how to get a man!"). But irrespective of the intention, the idea is, some good habits will be formed, based on the resolution of a new focus.

Practical Steps to The Formation Of Good Habits

Every day is a new wholesome 24 hour: Take charge!

Denzel Washington expressed in a quote how every day was symbolic of a man having 86,400 USD. If he loses $10 of it, he doesn't because of the pain of the money lost, throw the rest into the wind. In reality, the same 86,400 seconds is allotted to everyone globally at the dawn of every new day. Many unexpected events may occur probably due to your unpreparedness for the day, but here is the point where you take charge.

No matter the number of years past. The years you did not utilize due to lack of self-discipline or whatever reason it may be. It is not your fault. You did not know. Many people never get to open themselves to the greater success achievable in the future because they hold to the past errors till the end. Never being able to forgive themselves, they are riddled with shame, depression, and a fixed mindset that they can never achieve anything great. So instead of holding on to the long years they have left and letting go of whatever errors they might have made, they would instead hold on to the comfortable pain of not being enough.

So, the first step to breaking free and forming good habits that will propel success is taking charge.

Bury the past, and wake up from your drowning state to endless possibilities of this new day. The fact remains that "Every human can accomplish as much as she can dream." Many centuries ago, it was illogical to dream about landing a man on the moon. Though it took the effort of many generations laboring consistently to execute it, we eventually did it. A man landed on the moon! There is so much that you are capable of, and the truth is, the only person that can do what you can do, the unique way you can do it, is you.

Every new day is an avenue to do great things, achieve something great, make success happen, build, learn, try out something new, and live. Every new day is a part of a journey to the destination called your "ambition." So, begin now to forgive yourself for whatever mistakes and formidable errors you may have committed. You honestly did not know. However, now you do know. And now you will take charge.

This is the most valuable lesson in getting out of your box. Whatever success models you will create is best rooted in the idea that "As long as I am alive, I can achieve my goals. I deserve them, and I will achieve them". Your mind is now free to tap into your inner reservoir.

Start the Day Early!

The energy you put into the early hours of the day says a lot about how the day will go. Several people do not get out of their beds thirty minutes after they first open their eyes in the morning. "The sheet feels warm and nice, and the morning is cold." Some others will even dare to say "there's no work today," and for whatever reason you give yourself, to not get up early enough and make the most of your judicious morning energy; you've probably lost out that consistency charm that sparks up from a great morning strength.

Procrastination is one of the main struggles with this present generation. Many distractions empower this great enemy as well. Fortunately, the solution to procrastination begins with what you do with your morning.

Many people believe that procrastination is a delay in heavy, monotonous tasks. Office projects or assignments should have been done since the beginning of the holidays or the weekend. People fail to realize that procrastination begins from not standing up from bed when you wake up and delay making breakfast till you are hungry. Procrastination is a habit that dwells on comfort—lying on the couch doing nothing productive.

To defeat procrastination would mean to start taking note of the little things that may seem unimportant—brushing your teeth at the right time – early. Taking your bath and setting out to making the most of your morning.

Don't Look to Breaking Bad Habits; Focus on Overwriting Them With Good Ones

When washing a cloth, our goal may be to remove the cloth on the cloth and reveal its sparkling glow. Our action is to overcoat the cloth with a cleaner medium, through which the dirt is flushed out of the fabric and forgotten. Water and probably detergent are the agents used to make the cloth clean. You never see a person intending to washcloth by just rubbing the dry fabric against each other. This is what creating good habits feels like.

Procrastination is solved by getting up in time to get the job done. Being dirty is solved by taking a bath; a poor music skill is resolved by extensive practice and guide. You have to counter the bad habits with a new one.

Addictions are one of the most common habits that people try to break away from. Often you hear people say, "I've tried everything to make it stop; I just can't break away from it." Well, if you have been trying to break away from it and it's not working, don't you think clinging on to a freedom mindset would be a better option?

Breaking off from addiction in every place that has worked has been more about holding on to something else.

Set up Actual Success Models

People don't become wealthy by declaring boldly that "I am financially enriched." As convenient as that may sound, it just never works. To get rich, you have to work.

This is the idea. Most times, people want to become rich so that they can afford everything they ever desired. Not a bad thing! But the downfall of that is that becoming wealthy by accident (say they win the lottery, for example) only opens their eyes to the things they always wanted to get. Without the skill of wealth multiplicity, they soon go back to being broke, or worse, in debts.

To become rich, just like any other ambition that a person desires to have, one must follow the flow process.

1. **Acquire knowledge:** Knowledge is the proper route to take to achieving anything. In drafting a success model, the individual must get as much information as possible. This information is obtained from books, meditations, talks, conferences, and formal and informal education. All information is relevant and would help you achieve your goals in one way or another.

2. **Go through the process:** This is where you internalize the information you are gathering and impact your unique creative power into it. Note that everyone is capable of creating. This is why you must sit down and draw out your battle strategy towards reaching your goals. This process

may also require you to talk to people who have carted farther ahead to a greater extent on their waters. Listen to their input and modify your plans. Fill every loophole, question yourself on the 'how,' 'when,' and 'why' you want to do what you want to do. This is enough to stir you up to the final phase.

3. **Execute the plan:** Everything you have done to this point is NOT worthless even if it is not eventually executed. Don't let anyone scourge you with the failure mentality. The plan could be executed by your son in some years to come, or by anyone else. So, kudos for a job well done. However, you must see this one through. Despite the fact, your satisfaction with what you've done till this point is guaranteed, but I don't think you would have gone this far reading this book if you were one to settle with less.

Get up and execute your plans. It is your plan! It is your creative power! Your child can build on your establishment. That is a better legacy to offer a man than a plan on a sheet of paper.

Good Habits Are Recreated Daily

Once you have structured your success model, it is advisable to break it down into bits and work it out daily. Remember always that the idea of making progress is to consistently repeat the right things and the productive things you have given yourself to every day until it becomes a part of you. If you are working against poor hygiene, draft out a hygienic structure that would cover your bathing and skincare routines, properly balanced diet plans, cardio or muscle training exercises, or whatever plan you decide for yourself. Consulting professionals, even at a financial cost, is worth it.

Do your routines daily. As in a battle, you overwrite the bad habits with the good ones, one day at a time, until the good habits completely overtake you. Good habits channeled at whatever is known by their distinction to always set people up for success. So, the idea is doing the same things over and over every new day until you get rid of the bad habits altogether.

Your Success Journey Is Yours Alone and Not a Race Against Someone Else

Often, we may feel defeated by trying so hard, and the other person is doing so little yet achieving much, especially in the financial race, to getting more money. The first thing to note in this wise is that you can trust the process. Even people who had their successes handed over to them by the positive nepotistic power of their wealthy celebrity parents or their politician friend still have to work hard daily to keep that success.

Your race is yours alone. And the only person worth comparing your progress with is yourself.

How do you do this?

Easy. Get a journal or a notepad and document your progress. Every day, you will write the plans and targets to be executed and achieved at the end of the day. At the end of each day, you will write the reviews and tick the boxes. This book helps you keep track of your plans and execute them properly.

Chapter 10: Outline Of How Habits Are Formed: Signal- Habit- Gratification

Often, we hear people emphasize how essential it is to build good habits. Right from the first grade till probably a time of our lives, they cannot walk up to us to say it any longer. A lot of people have come to understand the benefit of a good consistent habit. And while they may continue struggling with the old unhealthy habits, they still acknowledge that consistent good habits are undoubtedly valuable. Nonetheless, this has not helped them resolved the old bad habits.

To be able to reshape habits, an individual must first understand how it is formed. It is synonymous with every and any other thing in our day to day lives and even professionally in our jobs. To get better at a game, you must first understand how it works.

The physiology, behavioral pattern, cognitive skills, and baseline habits are shaped generally by two life factors: the inherited genetic traits (nature) and the environment (nurture). The make-up of a man that allows him to act the way he does, think the way he does, and speak the way he does is both a function of his genetic make-up and the environmental factors around him. So, while we grew up, we recognize that nature and nurture had a delving impact on the inherent skills and habits we built. These impacts were, however, still not the real deal. We may have seen people without a musical family background, who grew up in a society where music or musical instruments were not appreciated or propelled. They accidentally encounter a musical instrument on day zero, and on day 200, they are perfect with the rudiments, intermediacy, and some level of professionalism on the instrument. Given another 200 days, they have perfected the instrument. The events that happened between Day zero and day 200 is not tied to genetics or environmental conditioning; the power of habits is what shaped this person to distinctively master an instrument efficiently in a period some people might call "short."

In the study of evolution, Jean-Baptiste Lamarck created a law of use and disuse. This law may not seem relevant in discussing how habits are formed, but one law encouraged neuroscientists to look at the body in a whole new direction.

The law explained how organisms had a natural tendency towards perfection. That the consistent use of an organ in a particular way would develop it to suit the condition or activity perfectly, it is required for. The latter part of the law was Lamarck's proof that these developed organs or traits are now uniquely passed to their offspring (explaining how the giraffe got its long necks and limbs). But this latter part is not the point. The point is, Lamarck was able to recognize the idealism behind habits.

He may not have known it perfectly, but he was in every way right about the natural tendency of humans towards perfection. Habits are formed by consistent repetition of an action or activity in a particular way.

So generally, the basis of habit formation is the consistent repetition of action over some time. By the law of use and disuse, Lamarck further explained that the organs (or the dominant half of our body), which we use most consistently, would get stronger and more skillful; the neglected ones eventually die out. This law's impact might not be seen physiologically in the human body until a long seen most actively in habits that we build.

The habits we emphasize are built better and more perfectly. And when they are neglected, we go from being rusty to losing the level of perfection we had long attained on the skill.

Signal, Habit, Gratification

When neuroscientists, psychologists, and other professionals of behavioral medicine found the cases of viral encephalitis patients who, after surgery, lost their memories and several Amnesia patients who, while in their homes, could stand up and locate the bathroom when they were pressed or walk from the sitting room to the bedroom without getting lost; they knew there was much more going on within the cerebral cortex than we had believed. These patients were people who could not tell you the food they ate the previous night or how you got to be sitting with them in their houses. They had nothing; nonetheless, somehow, they were able to navigate their entire house, cook whole meals, several chores without any evident complication in their memory bank.

This made neuroscientists design the rat-and-cheese experiment, understand how this could be possible, and how much it could be utilized to treat these mental eases, and understand the power of habits.

The selected lab mice were operated on for over five hours with minute neurosensory transmitters placed on their brain to begin the study. This neurosensory transmitter could detect brain activity in waveform and transmit the results data to a computer where it was being evaluated and studied.

At the onset of the experiments, the rats were placed at one end of a dark enclosed T-shaped tunnel, locked behind a barricade, and a cheese bar at the curved left-hand end of the tunnel. A timer was set, and with a loud bang at zero seconds, the barricade was opened. The rat could perceive the smell of the cheese and would not navigate shrewdly across the tunnel. This experiment was carried out on several rats, repeatedly daily, for several months.

The first few weeks of the experiment showed the rats scurry carefully from right to left of the tunnel. Colliding with the walls of the tunnel and making slow progress across the tunnel. The sense of proprioception was not keen, and so they couldn't sense their position against the cheese they so desired.

After the first few weeks, the rats collided less with the tunnel wall and moved to the cheese at a shorter time duration. Finally, at the end of the experiments, the rats, upon the loud bang that opened the barricade, will dash at full speed to the cheese's precise location.

With this experiment, the neuroscientist and psychologist were able to prove one basic thing amidst numerous others. The most inspiring rationale behind the formation of a habit is gratification.

In the experimental design, the loud bang was the signal. Signals today are sensations that bring about an action. Hunger or the need to urinate is a typical example of signals. These signals set us into a habitual motion to decide whether we like or not to gratify food or a relieved bladder.

This is where habit formation gets interesting. Our response to those signals that we received, in the exact manner of response, brings about habit.

Not getting up immediately from the bed to use the restroom whenever you are pressed is a suppressive habit formation. It teaches the brain to relieve the urgency of the signal. And though it may have long-term damaging effects on the body (particularly on the urinary tract), the habit formed around that signal is suppression.

Habits can be so precise and perfected that they are done with the least activity of the brain. For example, Tyler Mclaughlin is an English boy that juggles. He started learning how to juggle at the age of five. And while it may have taken him fifteen years to master the craft, he now combines juggling with so many other mental processes like taking a call, riding a bike, and several other things.

The idea is this, and the human brain is composed of many compartments judiciously serving different purposes. The cerebrum and frontal cortex engage in tedious tasks and creative thinking processes. They resolve on decisions to problems and create new foundations for new habits. Now, as the brain gets efficient in delivering a task, it utilizes lesser brain activity. Soon, at the mastery of the task and consistency, the part of the brain that regulates such function becomes a smaller, but not any less potent area, the basal ganglia. The basal ganglion is the area for arousal, some limbic functions, and very importantly, the execution of tasks 'too simple' for the brain to stress about.

For example, sweeping or driving a car. They are often controlled by the same region of the brain, the basal ganglion. The human mind builds so much of a habit around it that it becomes too easily navigated. The essence of this is to give room for more tasking activities.

Thus, in the case of the patient with retrograde Amnesia (memory loss) manifested after his viral encephalitis operation, he was able to locate the bathroom quickly and cook whole dishes without any complications or a noticeable defect in his brain because this was a habit that had been done consistently over the years and was no longer controlled by the cerebrum, but by the basal ganglion. The basal ganglion is not affected by amnesia since it is a disease that affects the cerebrum.

Chapter 11: Self-Image

What crossed your mind when you flipped the book and opened this chapter? Did you happen to depict what self-image could mean? Did you try to picture the little you standing in front of a mirror in admiration?

Self-image is simply a mental picture which is hardly subject to change. It portrays not just your physical features such as height, hair, weight, etc.). Still, also elements that you have overtime learned about yourself either from your personal experience (strength, weaknesses, abilities, etc.) or what you think about yourself from other people's perspective.

Your self-image is a perspective you have about yourself; it is more like the internal encyclopedia that tells you all you think and know about yourself. It is what makes you believe in a certain way about you. It makes you see yourself as pretty, smart, lazy, greedy, etc. The image of yourself is paramount because it helps you think about yourself, understands yourself, and enables you to interact with yourself and the outside world.

Have you ever noticed that you judge yourself based on these three things? Your physical appearance (How do I look?), Relationships (Am I valued?), and Performance (Am I doing enough?)

A healthy self-image is when you think about yourself; the images and feelings that follow are pride and importance.

How you see yourself can emanate from either of the following;

- How you see yourself

- Other people's perspective of you

- How you interpret the judgment of other people about you

- How you perceive yourself

Research says these four ways of self-image perspective may not be an accurate description of a person. All, some or none could be true.

In the terminology of cognitive and social psychologists, self-image is called "Self-schema." According to them, self-schema heaps up knowledge or information and influences the way you think and recall. It is also referred to as the traits in which you use to define yourself.

How Your Self-Image Evolved And Two Types Of Self-Image

The image you have about yourself developed over time due to the things you have learned. Early childhood factors such as our parents, nannies, guardians, teachers, etc. played a major part in your self-image. These relationships played a role in shaping your mind. All of these have also built on what you call your strengths and weaknesses.

Negative Self-Image

The negative image emanates from criticisms you have over time since you were a child down to your current growth stage. Such a view has a way of eating deep into you that you begin to believe in them, thereby damaging what you think about yourself.

As a child, you would be more vulnerable to accepting negative opinions and judgments from higher figures such as your parents, elders in your neighborhood or community, and other significant others. You were more vulnerable because you were just a child and could make little or no decisions for yourself compared to now. You had to accept those judgments and opinions because they came from people you looked up to for life; you had no competence or ability to process and evaluate them.

Growing into the adolescent stage of life, you might have suffered from "body shaming" when the opinion of other people about your physical appearance takes a toll on you and makes you uncomfortable about your body. People who lack or have a low sense of self are usually prone to developing a social disorder.

Typically, someone who has a negative self-image usually has the following mentality;

- Excessively critical

- Compare one's self with others, especially peers

- Negative self-talk

- Believes that anyone who gives a positive compliment is telling a lie

- Always see one's self as a failure

Factors That Contribute to a Negative Self-Image

- **The beauty values and norms of society:** Every society has its core values, regulations, ethics, taboos, etc.; some societies have a definition of an idea or a perfect shape. Often, if you do not meet up to your society's "body expectations" of your society, you automatically have this negative image.

- **Personality:** Many people always have this very high expectation of themselves to a point where they begin to set unrealistic goals. They have this perfectionist mindset that does not give any room for a grade "B." They want the perfect height, slim waistline, bulging hips, broad, muscular chest, etc. This category of people usually has a negative self-image when they do not meet the required goals or when their bodies are not aligning with the mental picture they have in their heads. Do you have this personality type? You can only be a failure if you stop trying, give room for yourself.

- **Childhood experiences:** In a situation where an individual had a very critical childhood could birth a negative self-image. He or she was always being criticized more than they were ever appreciated. Such criticisms come from parents, teachers, friends, etc., such experiences tend to develop and even worsen if not taken care of. Do you attest to this?

- **Illness**: Someone with a chronic disease or genetic disorder usually have this negative opinion of self. He or she feels less privileged and unwanted. Also, people going through a mental illness like depression, trauma, anxiety disorder, etc. often have this negative opinion.

A negative self-image makes you focus on your limitations, flaws, failures, etc. understand that there is always a way out and a beautiful side to every story.

Positive Self-Image

Just as the title implies, a positive self-image is simply having a good feeling, view, and impression about yourself. When you see yourself as a happy and healthy person, see yourself as a desirable and attractive personality, affirm that you are the ideal version of yourself, agree with all the beautiful qualities you have, agree that others think highly of you the way you think highly of yourself then and then can it be said that you have a positive image of yourself.

When you possess positivity in how you see yourself, it gives you the ability to distinguish between your strengths and weaknesses, perfection, and flaws.

Creating and Maintaining a Positive Self-Image

Human behavior is always liable to change, and so is your self-image. Dynamism in the way you see yourself is very much learnable. Building a positive one begins with learning to accept and love yourself and accept the love of those around you.

Here are some ways to create and maintain a positive self-image:

- Describe or define what your personal goals are. Are they attainable, realistic, and measurable?

- Avoid comparing yourself with other people.

- Take charge of your thoughts; avoid negative thoughts about yourself.

- Record successes and give yourself a treat for that.

- What are the things you love about yourself? Write them out.

- Converse with your inner child; rule out negative thoughts about yourself and replace them with positive ones.

- Build on your strengths and inner abilities.

- Speak positive affirmations to yourself, and they go a long way.

- Love yourself; if you don't love yourself first, you cannot recognize and accept the love of others.

- Maintain friendship with positive individuals and let go of toxic ones.

- Exercise.

- Let go of your past and take time to heal.

- Rewrite your self-history, erase the negativity of other people.

- Take your self-image into account.

In the conclusion of this chapter, you would give a thumbs up if it is stated that "having a positive self-image is gold in itself." Your positive image of yourself helps you to gain confidence, achieve goals, live a good/healthy life, and experience the fulfillment of your dream.

Chapter 12: How Anticipating Gratification on the Signal Forms Habits

There is a common cliché that if you perform the same action consistently for 21days, you will be addicted to doing the action. This is somewhat true; addictions and habits are formed by always doing the same thing repeatedly.

The Science of Habits Formation

The human brain works amazingly, and one of the reasons your body adapts to certain habits or actions is because of your mind. Have you ever set the alarm to wake you up every 5 am? After a few days, if you have consistently obeyed the alarm, your brain and body will begin to adapt to the change. Have you ever wondered why this happens?

Our brains form a connection, called the neural pathways connection, and these connections happen between the neurons of the brain. The neurons then get stronger each time you perform a task, and the more we perform a task, the better it becomes. The more we repeat that same task, the easier the task becomes for us to get it done, and it becomes a habit.

On the other hand, habits can be formed whenever a form of gratification or pleasure is around the corner.

The truth is your brain feels better when there is instant gratification rather than a long term gratification. What do I mean? How many times have you ended up surfing the internet binge-watching Netflix when you were supposed to read a book, prepare for a test, or complete your assignment? Or how many times have you chosen to eat junk food, and drink carbonated drinks over water, even though you know that those kinds of food are not healthy enough for you? If you are wondering why you do these things, well, your brain has a few facts to explain to you.

According to research from the University of Princeton, they are two areas of the brain. The first area is associated with emotions and is more attracted to instant gratification than others, while the second area is connected with logical reasoning. Based on these two areas, you can donate that our brain is always active and responsive to instant gratification such as sleep, eat, play games, watch a movie, and engage in any form of playful and easy activities. While your logical aspect gives you reasons why you must take the actions, in the face of actions, you are mindful of the consequences, the aftermath, and the things that you can benefit from your actions.

Now, the sad reality about these two parts is that they conflict with each other. That is why you cry and frown when your alarm rings. That is why you shout when you are asked to work on your assignment. Of course, you understand that your performance is important, and your performance at school will help you later in life, but you would prefer to party, play with your friends, or skip classes for no reason. The winner of the conflict depends on you as an individual. Like I always say that your will or choices are not independent of your choice and desire. You cannot make any form of choice without you first knowing what you want.

However, you can use the emotional part for your benefit. What does this mean? Having understood that these two areas of your brain are always conflicting, you should pay attention to your brain's emotional part.

How can this be done?

How about you create an incentive for yourself for every task you need to complete at work? The moment goals you achieve, the more results and incentives, and this way, you can be happy with yourself.

How to Form Habits

- **Be flexible enough:** Remember, they are your habits and not for someone else. So, don't be too hard on yourself. Of course, the habits are to make you better but try to be flexible enough.

- **Start small:** there is a saying that little drops making the big ocean start with a stone, then two stones, then three, and then a pack of stones. The goal is not quickly become a master of habit but to ensure that you are productive even with the habits.

- **Be consistent:** consistency is critical, and never trade it for anything. The reason why you can become a master of a habit is to remain consistent. Do the same thing every day, at the same time, and experience productivity and creativity.

Your habits are powerful, just like the foundational blocks often not seen in houses; they help you stand firm and right. Like I will always say, every successful man has invested heavily in tons of habits.

Chapter 13: The Key Habits

*"Our character is the collections of our habits. Because they are consistent, often unconscious patterns, they constantly, daily, express our character." – **Stephen Covey***

My key habit, which is reading, brought the following benefits to me: increase in vocabulary and comprehension, empowers me to empathize with other people, aids in sleep readiness, reduces stress, lowers blood pressure and heart rate, fights depression symptoms, and prevents cognitive decline as I age. To date, it is still my number one key habit of getting things done in every aspect of my life.

The need to get smarter, think wider, and get better can not be overemphasized when it comes to life and greatness. This need is not met by wishes or pity, and it is met by the right position and posture of the heart. The key habits or keystone habits are habits that make it easier to achieve your goals. These habits are key not because of their complexity but simplicity. Charles Duhigg defined keystone habits as "small habits that people introduce into their routines which unintentionally influence other aspects of their lives."

When planning for a holiday, we always have different paths that can take us to our residence. Some paths are far in the distance than the other, which can be convenient or rough. Normally, every sane man will go for an easy-to-follow and fast way, which will bring convenience into the rest of their journey. You may decide to play an easy route to achieve your goals and transform your life in the same vein. This route is no other than key habits. Key habits create a powerful effect leading to new actions, behaviors, and habits. You can't achieve all your goals once, and no man is designed to operate like that. I am not talking about simpler goals requiring the same working principles now, and I am talking about goals with their modus operandi. Each requires your hundred percent attention. If you try to achieve this type of goal once, the probability of it being fruitful is less than one. You can choose to get things done intentionally by creating your essential habits and do more with less energy. Keystone habits create a transformative effect that changes every area of your life.

Some Examples of Keystone Habits

- **Exercise:** It helps to have high levels of discipline and self-control, avoid procrastination, and avoid eating what the body doesn't need.

- **Sleep:** People who sleep poorly will struggle to learn better since the brain will be clogged with stress and find it hard to have a retentive memory. Moreover, sleep deprivation leads to instability; hence people who sleep less find it challenging to make decisions. According to a medical thesis from the Harvard Medical School, *"Sleep deprivation makes our attention, focus, and vigilance drift, making it difficult to receive and understand information. Without adequate sleep and rest, we overwork our neurons, leading to neuron dysfunction, causing a lack of coordination and inability to learn new things."*

- **Keeping a diary:** Writing about your stressful day will help you reduce stress and, at the same time, improve your writing and thinking skills.

Identifying your keystone habits that meet these criteria and suit your lifestyle is important. It must be on your terms though that doesn't mean you should not go for the best. If you are struggling to find any, there are some examples below:

Make your bed in the morning, clean your room, pray, donate money to a charity monthly, spend time with loved ones, play a musical instrument, draw, write, or paint.

These examples, among many others you can find, will make it easy for you to find your keystone habits. Once you select your keystone habits, different strategies can help make it easier to get along with them for a long time. They include: starting small, creating a favorable atmosphere for it to work, and scheduling your habits.

Benefits Of Key Habits

- **Increased commitment level:** There is no way you would consistently act for two months that it won't get stuck in your consciousness. There is a way the mind works such that when you, through discipline, programmed it for a cause, it will get addicted to it to the extent where you won't need an external force to remind you of doing it. There will always be a nudge from within when the time to remind you. It will get to a level where you start feeling uncomfortable if you haven't done it, and you won't be comfortable until you do it. This is the reason why negative habits are hard to break because the soul is already aligned to it; it does it. Naturally, you don't need to remind it again. Imagine developing a key habit, your level of commitment to other causes will increase because you have learned how to be committed in a simple but effective way.

- **Cause positive change:** A key habit is a catalyst for positive change. If you want to embrace diet and reduce your body weight, let your key habit be a person working out. The lesson and the determination you learn during this period will be a massive and effective threshold for you when there is an important goal you want to achieve. You already have a habit that is made for it, and you just go for it. You won't know the importance of saving the lowest currency as a key habit until you have a big project at hand or some goals that need your financial commitment. The thing is a key habit that leads to a positive change, which will lead to another better positive change. Just one key habit. We have kids who will never eat out because they have been raised to eat at the table with their family; they are always prudent in spending.

- **Gives self-image:** A boy's handwriting is not good, and in the quest to help him, he was taking self-image lessons from his teacher. He did this for more than one year, and his writing got better. But little did the teacher know that her quest to help the boy improved in his writing has caused an inner change in him. The boy's confidence soared; he now sees himself in a good self-image. If he can practice all that he does not know, he will get better. A key habit of writing images has led to the boy obtaining a good self-image. Same for meditation, it has its massive advantage.

Transform your life using keystone habits; without them, everything seems to fall apart. With them, everything becomes easier and more effective. Be ready to stand up and create the habit you need to be successful in life.

Chapter 14: Find the Key Habit That Reprograms You According to Weber and Fechner's Principle of Minimum Stimulus Law

Weber and Fechner's Law Principle is associated with human perception and how it is related to the changes that occur between physical stimulus and perceived change. These changes include the stimuli to the five sense organs, the eyes, the nose, the tongue, the ears, and the skin.

The law establishes the response's proportionality, not to the stimulus but the logarithm of the stimulus. As long as I apply large stimuli, the Response will first be proportional and smaller and smaller. When I apply the threshold stimulus So, the response is 0. Things get interesting when I apply Stimuli with a value between zero and the Threshold Stimulus value. I will have very large responses in these cases, proportional to the logarithm of S/So, facing inwards and tending to infinity.

The area in which we must work to create the key habit is, therefore, the one with So values (= 1 in the graphic example), where small Stimulus, which we can identify as actions, corresponds to Reactions (change) of considerable value and inward-facing. This is useful for the living organism to modify itself internally. The smaller the stimulus between 0 and So, the bigger the reaction.

Here Is an Example

A patient visits the doctor for medical tests and routine. The doctor makes him sit on the couch to check his reflexes. With the orthopedic hammer, he gives a first light blow to the patient's knee, who, under normal health conditions, reacts by raising his leg, i.e., reacting towards the outside. Afterward, a slightly more decisive blow, and the patient reacts faster. Finally, from a powerful blow, and the patient breaks his knee (do not try at home, believe me) with an immediate reaction equal to 0. If, instead, he had applied a very small (minimum) Stimulus, with a value between 0 and So, the Response would have been of a great motion value, tending to infinity, without the patient raising the knee but facing the inside of the knee. That is, the organism tends to give a response inside the knee. It is not a case if therapies in which minimal stimuli are applied, such as Tens current, acupuncture, acupuncture, therapeutics, topical drugs, i.e., explicitly directed on the part to be treated, are recognized by official medicine as therapies indicated for countless pathologies. This fascinating physics principle has innumerable implications that are part of in-depth studies dealt with in other publications.

Perhaps, you cannot relate to this example well. Here is a breakdown of how Weber and Fehncer works and how they can be connected to habits.

When someone pinches you, at that moment, your brain receives the feeling and interprets the pinching; thus, you feel pain. As a form of reaction to the pain, you may cry or retaliate immediately. However, this chapter is focused on key habits that reprogram your mind according to the law.

If you are a fat person who wants to lose some pounds, you will most likely choose to exercise and maintain a healthy diet. Because you are on the verge of weight loss, your key habits will include regularly exercising and dieting.

The big question is, how can they affect you based on the laws? When you exercise regularly, you instruct both your body and mind that it can be fit. At the same time, because you have instructed your mind about your goals, you will find it challenging to eat inappropriate foods.

Moreover, another fact that this law is pointing to us is it is very easy to master a habit that has a direct impact or influence on your five sense organs.

- Tongue: Less talking, less eating
- Ears: Active listening

- Skin: Practice your skincare routine more

- Eyes: Only feed your eyes with essential and relevant information.

In conclusion, every habit can reprogram your life. You should invest more in healthy habits.

Chapter 15: Because We Are Lazy

Laziness happens at some point in the life of every human, and you aren't an exception. Can laziness be classified as a personality, trait, habit, or even behavior? Laziness arises as a result of so many things. Humans generally have different personalities and traits. Personalities who are less persistent would likely be its first prey.

Laziness could have varying interpretations, lack of interest in doing anything, no motivation, unwillingness to complete tasks, etc. In other words, laziness could arise due to a person's lifestyle, physical issues, or psychological problems such as depression, fear, or even anxiety.

Just like an insect, it creeps into your mind and holds you hostage. It walks into your life and begins to order you around. It even sometimes deceives you into thinking that you deserve to take a break, and then you'd start taking breaks. It then fully dominates and becomes a part of you. It is the greatest enemy of taking steps.

Why We Are Lazy

Why do you suddenly fail to do what you are supposed to even when you have all it takes? Having a good knowledge of it and everything that comes with it would help you shoot it from a distance before it gets to you. However, let's see why we are lazy.

- **Distraction:** While you are at your job, many things could just pull you away from your job, making you think you will get back to it later. Sometimes, you could be bothered about something which may make you automatically lose interest in doing anything, and you may feel hungry and go in search of food; after eating, you might feel drowsy and tell yourself you would get back to work later. Would you get back to work?

- **Poor decision making:** Making decisions for yourself makes you feel responsible, accountable, and in charge of your life. When your mind is rarely made up, and you let other forces control you, you would always end up feeling lazy to do anything for yourself, even to the point of making decisions.

- **Depression:** There is always this unwillingness and loss of hope in a depressed heart. This state of mind often causes laziness.

- **Procrastination:** There are strength and willingness that comes with doing things immediately. When you tend to postpone the things you deed to do over and over again, you breed laziness. You even sometimes tell yourself it is not urgent and can be done later. If you postpone little tasks like sweeping your room, washing your clothes, doing your dishes, the 11th-hour miracle might not work for you when you have more serious things to do. With time, you would hardly be able even to complete bigger tasks.

- **Your lifestyle:** Living a disorganized life often gives room for laziness. When you sleep, eat, go out without any planned routine or list of things you wish to achieve for the day. Some people sleep as late as 2 am streaming videos online, and then they wake up very late in the morning feeling tired and too weak to do anything like a victim. When you have no planned routine, any event can just come up, and you'd embrace them; it often makes you give room for more pleasurable things and left you neglecting important things that also need your attention.

- **Motivation and accountability:** Being accountable to a group of individuals or someone motivates you to do something. The absence of priority and significance of what you are supposed to do would automatically kill your motivation level.

- **Too much workload:** When you have many tasks to complete, thinking of them alone can be discouraging. You automatically feel like doing nothing because you feel you have too much to do already. It shuts motivation or tolerance to complete any task, so you would rather just sleep.

Curbing Laziness

Now that you have been able to identify some doorways to laziness, how can this door be shut to a very good extent in your life?

- **What is the real problem:** One of the first things to do when you spot laziness from a distance is trying to figure it out like a puzzle? Do you feel too overwhelmed by your task? Sick about it? Uninspired? Or is there just no energy? Of course, if you weren't ready to overcome laziness, your eyes and mind wouldn't be fixed in this chapter. After spotting while you feel the way you think about your task, find a way to rid it off.

- **Self-worth:** The worth you place on yourself and your plans go a long way in determining how much you would let laziness get in your way. You could check YouTube for inspirational speaking of valuing yourself and placing priorities on your goals. Speak positive affirmations to yourself, surround yourself with people who live a purpose-driven life. Value yourself and your goals.

- **Utilize your strength:** What do you think builds up your strength when you are setting your goals? When you focus on your strength, it helps to build your productivity.

- **Seek Help:** You might end up not doing anything if you keep trying to figure out things on your own. Some so many people are ahead of you and have achieved what you are trying to achieve. If you think your task is too complicated and that's why you are lazy, seek help. When you seek help, it increases your chances of getting things done and meeting people who are willing to help.

- **Organize yourself:** Have you ever imagined a year without a calendar? The calendar helps you know your age, helps schools plan their academic calendar, helps people celebrate their anniversaries, etc., in a nutshell, the calendar helps to give the world meaning. So also does planning yourself helps give essence to your life. Be able to set time for everything and strictly adhere to them. You can achieve this by drawing out a time table. What are the areas of your life you think you have to focus on? And what are the things you need to build on? If you have a diary, fine and if you don't, you could get one. Set your goals, works towards them, and leave laziness aside. Organization starts with small things like arranging your clothes into the box, dressing your bed, arranging your house, etc. This can help motivate you to work

- **Don't expect too much from yourself:** you would often set unrealistic long-term goals when you expect a lot from yourself. The weight of the things you need to do would choke you to a point where you do not even feel like starting anything. Avoid "self-perfection syndrome." Don't overwork yourself, don't be overly critical of yourself, appreciate your small wins, and steadily aim higher.

- **Live healthily:** Managing stress, eating well, and exercising can help build your psyche. It can build your motivation level, intellect, and energy to help you clear your desk. Avoid fatigue, eat, sleep and give your body appropriate rest when needed.

End Results of Laziness

Maybe after seeing the consequences of what might happen "because you are lazy," it would help wave it off. Well, here they are:

- **It destroys:** So many people have had mind-blowing ideas of businesses and setups, but laziness hindered them from putting it into action. But before they knew it, someone else, who was hardworking, got the same idea and acted on it faster. Have you ever been in this shoe? Have you also seized an opportunity, but you lost it because you could not meet up with the deadline. After all, laziness had its toll on you? How painful was it? Indeed, very painful. Laziness destroys opportunities, ideas, goal achievement, and even wealth.

- **Affects your health:** Laziness poses a huge defect to a person's mental health, just like any other defect. It is a disease in itself. One thing that helps your brain more active is when you engage it in tasks and activities; especially new ones. When you are lazy, your brain does not function as it should. It would take more time to process some information and even answer some questions, especially if they are figurative. Prevention is always better than cure.

- **It enslaves:** A slave usually had no right of their own; they sleep and eat only when told. Laziness does this to its prey; it always excuses why you shouldn't do anything for that time being.

- **Kills your dreams, ambitions, and purpose:** For every dream that would be realized, an aspiration that would be attained, and a purpose that would be fulfilled, it takes months or years of consistent building. When laziness is dominant in your life, the result would be dreams that are not backed up with actions, desires that can never be met, frustration, negativity, and stagnancy.

Chapter 16: Why We Are Procrastinators

Disputably, if you were taken to court prosecuted for procrastination, you would be guilty as charged. You just sometimes feel like you would get that job done later. Have you ever asked yourself why exactly you procrastinate? You could be avoiding or postponing your tasks for reasons ranging from; laziness, lack of interest, the task may seem too tedious, boring or difficult for you, negative feelings and thoughts as you try to make attempts, etc.

The Four Types of Procrastinators

There majorly four types of procrastinators; let us take a discourse on them;

- **The one who feels he/she is very busy:** There is this "busy" syndrome for this category. Being busy becomes their greatest excuse for not completing their tasks. They unreasonably choke them to-do-lists with loads of assignments, and instead of facing each task or just spell it out what they do not want to do anything, they feel they are not free enough. When you keep saying you are busy, it is a pointer that you do not want to do anything. Sometimes, you even get overwhelmed with the activities you have choked yourself with, and then you blame it on having so many important things to do. Are you busy, or you are avoiding something?

- **The one who keeps getting fresh ideas:** You are in this category when you keep getting new tasks but never complete any. You often aren't patient enough to complete them and see results. You are very good at taking action towards your ideas, but you lose interest or get bored in the long run.

- **The one who thinks he/she performs well under pressure:** If you are in this category of procrastinators, one of your greatest difficulty is starting your task; you most likely would have shortened the length of time to complete a particular task. Most times, this is because you are good enough, and you trust yourself to complete the task within ten minutes or less. You believe in the 11th-hour saving grace. Nevertheless, the hobby of pressurizing yourself is not advisable, and the best thing is to always do what you should at the right time.

- **The one who feels he/she is lazy to do anything:** Funny enough, these sets of procrastinators are not lazy in the real sense. They just think no interest in doing anything or are too tired. When they see that they have wasted enough time being lazy, they go tough to complete their tasks. If you are among these settings, what you really should do is to be sincere and compassionate with yourself. If you feel you don't have time to rest, get to rest; come back stronger to complete pending tasks.

Seven Reasons You Procrastinate

People procrastinate for different reasons, and below are seven reasons why you procrastinate.

1. **Perfection syndrome:** This is often an obstacle in your assignments. It is an excellent idea to do a perfect and clean job. However, you start inviting difficulties when you set unfeasible goals to achieve them. Pressure on yourself drains your productivity and effectiveness, and this would also lead to self-condemnation. Progress more important than perfection. Eventually, when you seek improvement, perfection would set in.

2. **Fear of failure:** Sometimes, you want to get things done, but you are afraid of messing things up, so you just leave them as they are. There is always no harm in

trying first; how do you figure out the big success if you never try something?

3. **No Goal:** When you have no goal or zeal for the things you want to accomplish, you won't take your tasks seriously. How do you see yourself in the next five years? What steps do you have to take to make this come alive? How bad do you want to be a success? Then why do you still procrastinate?

4. **The length and difficulty of the task:** This is also one discouraging factor. The ambiguity of the task is often discouraging even to start anything. It makes you question your skill and competence leaving you in an overwhelmed state.

5. **How do you begin your day?** Starting your day would define how much you postpone your activities. How long do you stay in bed when you wake up? What do you do immediately when you wake up? Starting your day by picking your phone may be a bad idea. Your little decisions make up how much you would fulfill your day's jobs.

6. **Indefinite deadline:** In this case, you would always tell yourself that you would get it done "tomorrow." The deadline is a key factor that motivates you to get things done. So, procrastination happens when it is not there.

7. **No motivation:** This can sometimes be your mindset playing tricks on you. All you need is a change of mindset. With your task in your head, you just lay on your bed or couch, feeling like doing nothing. You often seek motivation to complete your tasks when you need to control your mind and get things done.

Humans generally procrastinate so many other reasons, ranging from the inability to set priorities right, indecisions, disorganization, altered Neuropsychology, etc.

Overcoming Procrastination

The following tips are some suggestions to help you deal with procrastination;

- **Program your mind to see your tasks as attractive:** One basic reason you keep postponing your tasks is that they are usually unappealing to you. You could make your tasks more appealing by; making yourself see it as a challenge (how many chapters can you read in one hour?), make it fun (if you love music while working, you could leverage on that or if you love keeping your mouth busy as you do, you could leverage on that too. Just try out something).

122

- **Accountability:** Being accountable to someone keeps you very conscious of your pending tasks; it gives you the same feeling as setting a deadline for yourself. Do you have any like-minded people around you? It could be your friend, colleague. Or just someone who wants to see you grow and would motivate you. Both of you might even have the same tasks to complete, make a commitment to each other, and hold yourselves accountable. This would not just put subtle pressure or motivation on you, and it would help you enjoy and learn from your tasks rather than just rushing through.

- **Distractions and self-discipline:** There are so many things that could distract you in the middle of a task. For instance, you could be in the middle of a task that requires the internet, and then you see an exciting movie trailer or a friend drops a message. Your focus could easily shift; you then tell yourself that the task can always wait, and you probably never get to visit that task again, or it takes you a more extended period to get it done. Distractions can also come from within; avoid over-thinking or worrying about other things. They lengthen the completion of what you should do or even make you get bored in the long run. When it comes to avoiding distractions, don't say to yourself, "I can't say no," it is always better you shut them down entirely until you are done.

- **Assign the task to someone else:** You always cannot do everything by yourself. Don't ever try to play the superman role. Whenever a task is voluminous, or you feel you are tired, assigning it to someone else wouldn't be a bad idea. This way, it would ease you off the stress and pressure of thinking you have something to do.

- **Try multitasking:** Multitasking helps to maintain your level of motivation and energy. Give a specific time to each task as you complete them. This way, your tasks would seem more appealing, and you would be able to get more tasks done within a maximized period. However, if you are a type that cannot multitask, don't force it.

- **Give yourself deadlines:** One thing deadlines help you to do is that it puts you under a subtle pressure, challenges, and reminds you that you have something to complete at a given period. Without a deadline, you would feel you have all the time in the world when the clock is consistently ticking. After breaking your tasks into bits, set a date limit for completing each task. Achieving your goals becomes easier and faster when you set short-term goals rather than long-term goals. You feel less pressured, and motivation is sustained till the completion of your tasks. Also, be sure to appreciate yourself as you complete your tasks.

The bottom line about procrastination remains that it is one of your greatest enemies to all your life's accomplishments.

Chapter 17: Get Out Of Your Comfort Zone

Have you ever had to complete a task, but you just don't feel like doing anything? Your body is guilty of that feeling. One thing about the human body is that it likes to be cared for. It does not like to be stressed; it most times feels lazy to go the extra mile. However, what are your reasons for wanting to achieve your goals? For instance, an entrepreneur has a goal of making massive profits, so they set goals and take the practical step to the plans.

Your comfort zone is like a time bomb waiting to blow off every golden opportunity, which later leaves you in the pool of regret. Have you ever missed an opportunity? How was the feeling?

Why does the comfort zone exist in the first place? Why does your body struggle to maintain that space, that feeling of not doing anything when you very well know that you have to get things done? You just want that space all to yourself.

Reasons You Do Not Want to Leave Your Comfort Zone

Sometimes, you are okay with staying in a situation even when a part of you tells you it is wrong, but you probably still decide to stay because you are afraid of getting stressed or you are scared of failure.

- **Procrastination:** Procrastination is relative to laziness. You postpone all your activities because you need to rest. Then this goes on and on. It is all about your mindset. Goal getters recognize procrastination from a distance and shoot it in the head before it comes any closer.

- **Laziness:** It makes you feel double-minded and unstable. No true successful man has this laziness syndrome because they know it is just a trap. Laziness finds its prey and feasts on them. Just get up! That way, you have defeated laziness. You can start by walking around, skipping, or jogging. Make your routines flexible. Then get to business.

- **Low self-esteem:** Why do you often feel like you cannot when you really can? Why do you listen to the negative talks in your head and that of other people? Failure is proof

127

that you are doing something. Do you remember any of your accomplishments? Of course, it was the same. You looked at failure in the eye and accomplished that goal. What makes you feel like you cannot do it again? Learn from every "failure" and think of how you can utilize them as tools to succeed.

The reasons you do not want to leave your comfort zone are just fantasies, and your reality is taking action. Don't entertain these visitors.

Three Ways Your Comfort Zone Drains You

Abraham Maslow gave a famous quote that goes thus; *"Anyone can choose to go back to safety or forward to growth. However, growth must be chosen every time, and fear must be defeated every time."*

There is a goal to achieve, a success to accomplish, a purpose to fulfill your greatest enemies are the things that make you feel too comfortable. Emerging from them is the very first step to attaining your goals and getting the satisfaction you deserve. Note that the more you stay, the more you are drained. Here are some ways you unconsciously get exhausted:

1. **Loss of experiences and opportunities:** One thing that makes life exciting and beautiful is exploration! How well you prepare for opportunities would determine how well you will maximize them. If you never give that idea or concept a trial, you would not just lose opportunities, achievements, experiences, and growth. Create a passion for your activities; build on your strength. It would go a long way for you.

2. **It keeps you static:** As humans, there are plenty of stages to life. Crossing into every step means that growth has taken place for qualification into the next step. Arguably, there is no joy like when you are making evident progress in your life's endeavors. When you grow, it means you are making progress, and when you are making progress, it means you are taking grand steps to your goals. When you say you are growing, you can tell that some actions you have taken, some goals you have achieved, and some opportunities you have taken hold of. But how about the times you refused to step out? It's the exact opposite of all that you just read. When you don't make any moves, it merely means you are not progressing. In other words, you are static and limited to the happenings in the outside world. Those goals would be left untouched, and every opportunity that should have been yours would become that of the very person next to you.

3. **You would always settle for less:** Have you ever noticed that one dominant goal-getters are Zeal and Passion? There's just always this voice that tells them, "There is more, you for it." Staying in your lane would always condition you to settle for less. You are more than less; less makes you settle for a life that doesn't make you happy and instead fills you up with the "if I had known" syndrome. There's no harm in trying. Welcoming the enticement of what your body is asking for is a deadly virus for a goal-getter like you. Get up! Settling for less makes you "live" rather than "exist."

Seven Behaviors to Leave Your Comfort Zone

- **Go from less to more:** Now, it is time to make things happen. After making your list, start from the goals that seem more attainable and realistic. Start from the easiest tasks while you try to enjoy what you are doing. As you proceed, you should get fired up to complete other tasks. Psychology has proven this over and over again. The point is, just try something. However small they seem, as long as it is something you have been avoiding for some time, just make it happen. Tick each task as you complete it; tell yourself you are almost done. This would make you proud of yourself. You can drop the book in your hand, complete a small task you have been postponing and then come back to enjoy your read.

- **Don't stop moving:** You may not be aware of this, but that little task you just completed has pushed you a step higher. As you stay consistent in doing this, energy and confidence sets in, the zeal to do more overpowers the zeal not to. Go ahead to complete the second, third, fourth, fifth... and on and on. Move like your life depends on it. Move like you would get shot at if you stop moving. It would be hard, it would be tough, and it would be draining. Your body would signal to your brain that you should get some rest. Now, it is left for the zeal and strength in you to serve as a shield to that signal. As aforementioned, movement means you are growing, and growth means you are attaining your goals. How does this feel?

- **Create and accept challenges to push yourself:** There sure must be areas of your life you wish to improve on or a list in which you want all items to be ticked as "done" what are the things you think you are afraid of doing? What are the tasks you think you can never complete? There's just a thin line between you achieving them or not. "Your Decision" your self-confidence is oppression to your oppressor. Just go ahead.

- **Create a procrastination list:** What tasks have you been putting on hold? What excuses have you been giving yourself for not achieving them? They could be activities like re-arranging your room, creating a podcast, writing a blog post, creating a market strategy, etc. Whether big or small, write them out.

- **Get yourself a new space:** Sometimes, your environment could be why you feel more relaxed. There could be distraction factors such as your television, your friend or sister, social media, etc., discipline yourself enough to set these factors for a moment and make things happen. No one would ever understand why you did not do the things you ought to do at the right time. For instance, some students leave their hostels to go all the way to the school's library to focus on. What location can serve as your library?

- **Positivity:** Anyone or anything that makes you believe you are unable is negative. Do away with anything that signals negativity, including that inner voice. Train yourself, go in right in front of your mirror, and speak positive affirmations. You could even do a video and play it every time you feel down. Envision your words as you speak.

- **Talk to someone:** Discussing your heart out with a trusted person goes a long way in easing off tension. This person could be a good friend, clergy, mentor, relative, etc. Try sharing your burdens with them, and you would see the magic this would bring.

Let's wrap up this chapter by saying that the world needs your impact, and lives depend on your accomplishments. Good luck!

Chapter 18: Listen and Improve Your Inner Voice

Have you ever had conversations in your head? You are talking to yourself and, at the same time, responding to yourself. Your inner voice is responsible for that. It is that little and still voice that guides and directs through your life's achievements. There is just this conversation that happens in your mind consciously and unconsciously; you could term it as internal monologue, internal discourse, inner speech, self-talk, etc.

Whenever you have to make choices or effective decisions or take critical steps, your inner voice comes to your rescue. There are also situations you must have regretted because you did not listen to that still small voice.

Two Reasons You Ignore Your Inner Voice

1. **Low self-esteem:** One thing low self-esteem does is that it makes you feel less of yourself, no trust in your inner abilities, and no decision making ability for yourself. You tend to think that your opinions are not valid, and you are

afraid of making mistakes. So, you ignore your voice and let people make decisions for your own life. Low self-esteem leads to a lack of trust for yourself and the killing of your potentials. Also, the way you treat yourself is the way others would treat you.

2. **Fear and lack of trust:** When you tend to doubt easily, you will find it hard to recognize your inner voice speaking. Have you ever had to give a crucial answer to probably an exam question, and a voice keeps telling you the option "D" is the answer, but you are too afraid to fail, and then you begin to doubt. You must have been faced with other similar scenarios where your inner voice tries to bail you out, but you are too afraid to take the risk.

Trusting Your Inner Voice

Your inner voice is more like your intuition, your very heart. You cannot trust significant others in your life if you cannot entrust yourself. Having no trust in yourself could be very detrimental to you. You must understand your strength and weakness; I wonder how some people don't know what they are capable of. Knowing these help you handle different situations and even your thinking pattern. Trusting your inner voice is not just a path to fulfilling purpose; it is also a healing path. Some ways to trust your inner voice are:

Firstly, work on avoiding multiple thoughts in your mind. In other words, maintain decorum. The more you work on keeping calm and still on your inside, the more audible your inner voice becomes. You could even use meditation and breadth consciousness as a means to maintain silence.

Listen to Your Heart. Shovel every other thought aside and listen to your heart. You don't have to wait forever before you learn to listen to your heart. You don't have to wait till it is time to make huge decisions to listen to your heart. Start from the little choices you make every day, such as what clothing to put on, what bag to take out, what route to take, what to prepare for lunch, etc. As you listen, trust the answers you get enough to act on them. The more you do this, the more you trust.

Furthermore, you could even do a heart check. This would help you make clearer distinctions between your mind and heart. Your heart is very simple and answers your questions in that light. Engage in discourses with your heart, ask questions like "have you ever lied to me, why I feel sad at the moment, why do I feel this grudge?" Your mind is just there to help you understand what your heart is saying or what it wants.

Listening and Improving Your Inner Voice

You might get confused due to so many voices in your head trying to speak to you at a go. However, how do you spot this one voice?

Listed below are some means that would help you communicate with your inner voice like best friends who were separated for years but are now back together.

- **Search for patterns:** If you were asked to listen to someone close to you (friend, partner, parent, boss, etc.) with your eyes shut, you would be able to decipher that voice. This is because, over time, your mind has mastered the talking pattern of that person. It is also the same way with your inner voice. Study the difference in the way it speaks compared to other voices in your mind. When does it come in? Through what approach? How do you feel when you hear it speak? Recall the times you listened to your inner voice speak to you, but you decided to shrug it off, which got you into trouble.

- **Pay attention to what you feel:** One of the unhealthiest things to do to your mental health is storing emotions. Your emotions are a part of you, and they very well need your attention. When you are beginning to feel in a certain kind of way, don't push it aside. Focus on what you are feeling; what are your emotions trying to communicate with you? What do you sense and feel in you? You can even write them out and conclude what you have penned down.

- **Give room:** One of the ways you unconsciously shut your inner voice is ignoring or giving no place for it. Meditation is one way that would help it become more audible. Stay calm and quiet; all your mind should be focused on is hearing your voice speak.

- **Focus and tame your mind:** You have to be willing to hear your inner voice. Your willingness, attention, and sensitivity are key factors in this task. These factors are the major ingredients to hear that internal monologue. It might get confusing as you try to listen; so many voices would want to take over. Your mind would start to introduce different voices and even imaginations to your head. This is normal. There are generally many voices in your head due to your mind's random thoughts, warning thoughts, and then your inner voice. These voices then put you in a dilemma and prevent you from listening to your inner voice.

You have a duty to sieve noises and fog thoughts from your mind. Just how you sometimes wipe off your phone to help it function better is always a clear mind. Form habits of engaging in activities, think about your vision and goals. Avoid overcrowding your mind with unnecessary happenings. There is also something called your "fog thoughts." These are thoughts that hang around and are undefined. They consist of emotions; that is, the things that are bothering you with no specific solution. These thoughts can be complicated because it consumes your mind with unclear reasons. You should get a hold of these thoughts and try to process them clearly, so they don't pose as your inner voice. Many doctors in the field have given theories to suggest that the very first voice you hear is your inner voice. The reason being that it speaks before your mind has had time to process any other voice.

- **Dialogue:** At a point, it would get frustrating due to too much confusion and your indecisiveness as to which voice you should adhere to. Take out your time to stay calm, avoid any pressure, both internal and external. Try to reflect and begin to observe. Observe your energy, your mindset, your thoughts, etc. Converse with your inner voice, pressure it to become more audible. Stay calm and process everything in your mind, then you would hear it speak clearly. Intentionally start conversations, take walks, and enjoy the dialogue.

- **Trust your inner voice:** Have you ever spoken to a person, and the person makes you feel like he or she does not trust you? How did you think about it? You would have probably promised yourself not to ever speak with the person again concerning that issue. It is also like this with your inner voice. You tend to shut it when you continuously show distrust for it. But when you listen to it and take evident steps, you open your arms wide to it. You would notice that it would become more audible and more expressive to you.

In conclusion, listening and maintaining a good relationship with your inner voice would be a huge advantage. Your self-esteem would be built, and it would help you grow, save you from making mistakes, and, overall, help you achieve your goals.

Chapter 19: Search Your Purpose

"We must have a theme, a goal, a purpose in our lives. If you don't know where you're aiming, you don't have a goal."
—Mary Kay Ash

What am I meant to do? What gives my life meaning? How do I want to contribute to the world? The importance and essentiality of purpose have made it become the duty of man to search for it. It should be a life theme and goal for everybody who still has a breath in themselves. I use "it" because as fundamental as searching for purpose is, it is by choice. Though it is by choice, an average human is always willing to be committed to topics that will give direction and add peace to their lives. Many don't want to survive without purpose; they need the drive to sustain them during their trying times; they need a sense of fulfillment and a source of joy. Nobody should search for their purpose in an atmosphere of ignorance and an environment void of light. The need to get wisdom and understanding can't be overemphasized.

The reason for which something is done or created or for which something exists is the purpose, and it needs to search for. The "Search" in search for your purpose doesn't connote looking for what is lost in oblivion but "looking for your essence within you." You are looking for your essence within you, not outside. You are finding the reason why you exist from your inner drive and passion. You need a concentrated effort to search, and a search is an act of finding, finding within. Don't be confused by the use of "within you," it is used in this context as your subconsciousness and consciousness. This search should be devoid of emotion even if it has a role to play with time. You are searching for your purpose, not what the world tells you, not what your parents say, but what you exist for.

Without purpose, you'll feel stuck because a purposeless life always revolves around circles. Life purpose is similar to the compass that leads to a sailor of the oceans. In the same way, your purpose will keep you focused.

Dear friend, you must search for it. The purpose is beyond the boundary of your education, riches, influence, power though they all have a role to play and, at the same time, be a source of distraction, robbing you of your fulfillment and the joy that comes with it. It can be said that your purpose is the reason why you want to be involved in whatsoever you lay your hands on; it is the driving force of your life.

Why Search? Why Purpose?

In Dr. Myles Munroe's book "Spirit of Leadership," he told the story of a lion who lived among the sheep for many years and couldn't do what a lion does. It was said that the lion has been in the care of the sheep owner since it was a cub, and it was raised with the sheep. One day the sheep went to the river bank to drink, and the young lion was with them, and an older lion roared from the other side of the river. The sheep ran, but the young lion discovered the Lion roaring from the other part of the river looked like the shadow of itself, which was seen when drinking from the river. This was the beginning of self-discovery for the lion cub until the day it went to where it was and never returned to the sheep.

The young lion's purpose and potential were within, but it had been overshadowed by the mediocrity and lack of inspiration in its environment. I can't imagine what it is like to be a lion and live like a sheep for years, but this is how some people have lived. When the purpose is known, abuse of your existence is unavoidable. Search your purpose so that you don't live as a sheep when you are a lion. You don't bleat when you ought to roar. You don't want to rob the world of being a partaker in your uniqueness and essence, and our world needs you right now. I will be mentioning some reasons why you should ignite your desire to search for your purpose.

- **Fulfillment:** In life, your joy is paramount. It is safer to avoid things that would steal your joy and peace. Fulfillment is not about the reward you get from what you achieve; it is the joy and peace you get from positive feedback. I think it is safer to say, and your reward is the positive feedback of your effort, i.e., the result. When you search, find, and act on your purpose then, the fulfillment is immeasurable.

- **Maximizing identity and potential:** Nothing helps you maximize your identity and potential than a sense of purpose; it makes you responsible and selfless. Purpose makes you channel your potential in the right direction, and your identity will be utilized till you reach your peak. The purpose is also a revealer of hidden potential and crusher of low self-esteem. Knowing your purpose increases your value and self-worth.

- **Direction:** There is a sense of direction that comes with a sense of purpose. You don't do things because others are doing it; you are doing it because there is a goal you want to achieve, which is in alignment with your purpose. You don't follow the crowd anymore because your focus has been set like a flint.

Among others, these compelling reasons should spur you to search till you lay hold of purpose and live it as your reality. Search within, and this search can be synonymous with digging land to get a treasure. Dig because you are sure this treasure is in this land, in you, search with all assurance that you will seem. If you don't search, you won't find it. If you don't find it, you won't benefit from leading a purposeful life. Now you know why you must search, and the next step is to learn how to search.

How To Search For Purpose

1. **Believe:** You must believe in a thing before you can acquire it. You bought a phone because you believe it will meet your demand. Putting an effort to search for what you don't believe in is a futile approach; you are what you think. Searching for your purpose or purpose discovery is a process, and its unveiling comes in the layer. Believe is a significant agreement that purpose is essential and worth searching for.

2. **What can you do effortlessly?** We all have our strengths and weaknesses. We have needs we meet effortlessly and selflessly. Maybe it concerns us directly or indirectly. Needs that we want to meet all the time need we don't mind inconveniencing ourselves to meet. Selflessness is a great attribute of people who live purposefully. Look within, search your heart, that thing that gives you fulfillment though doesn't give you any financial reward may be the indicator you need.

3. **Identify your passion:** when I talk about passion in this context, I am not talking about being emotional; I am

talking about conviction. I am not talking about a means to an end, and I am talking about the end itself. I understand we have a unique quality or skill which we have a strong feeling for; we also love to do it. This is cool, but this is not it. They are a means to an end. For example, I have a passion for writing, but my greatest passion is to see people discover their purpose. I can say my purpose is to see people discover their purpose, and I will use every means to get this done. The purpose is the essence of the soul. Look within and find yours also.

After all has been said and done, Act! It may take some time, effort, and you may also need an older lion like the young lion I talked about earlier, to make you know you are a lion, not a sheep. If what it will cause you is to read, read. Suppose it causes you to retreat, retreat. Don't get this information and not act; nothing is too much to give in other to acquire something worth life fulfillment.

Chapter 20: Focus Only On Important Things

Whatever has your attention has your strength, zeal, and passion. Your ability to draw lines between what is necessary and what does not make you a goal-oriented person. Loss of focus majorly arises from three things; what you can see, touch, and think.

Some factors that make you lose focus include; phone, outings, gossip, the internet, noise, essential thoughts, etc. Can you identify with any of these?

Firstly, it is okay to admit that avoiding distractions is tough. Concentrating on a particular task for hours and denying yourself of some things just to get that task done. Nevertheless, if the purpose must be fulfilled, there is a need to take practical steps. Generally, everyone, at some point, gets distracted. Why?

Reasons You Get Distracted On Things That Can Always Wait

Distraction can arise due to your inability to pay attention, lack of interest in the activity from internal and external forces. Studies show that some individuals have these anxiety symptoms of being easily distracted, such as the difficulty to formulate thoughts, easily distracted than the norms, crash in thinking patterns, difficulty to focus, etc. Here are some prominent things that make you lose focus:

- **No self-discipline:** When you don't follow your to-do-list, it is as good as not having one at all. You wake anytime you like, sleep late, etc., indiscipline always brings about disorganization, and disorganization produces little or no productivity.

- **Internal factors:** These two factors are responsible for taking away your focus. Internal factors consist of your mindset. It is a task to bring your mind together and give it enough strength for work. One good method of bringing your mind together has a workspace; it could be in your room, balcony, or anywhere you find okay. Arrange your tools and get ready; your mind would fall into place. Avoid taking breaks in your workspace so that it won't be more like a playground. Remember, your mind is taking notes.

- **External factors:** Don't forget your external factors; they comprise the physical things you love to do or even your favorite persons. Whether you like it or not, this factor is very much present and even more unavoidable than your internal factors. Sometimes you have this pressing task to complete, and the zeal is just there! Then your best friend puts a call through. Try to make up for the time spent on these factors.

How to Deny Distractions

Have you ever seen a surgeon in the operation room (maybe in the movies) or an artist painting a picture? What have you noticed? They pay apt attention because they know the costs of any slight mistake. What could your slightest mistake cost you, and how do you overcome them?

- **Take breaks:** You probably would find this point ironic. Yeah, take breaks. Sometimes, your body would break down when you overwork yourself, leaving you unable to complete any task. Don't overwork yourself; take time out to rest. Understand your body type and work with it. This strategy is simply for the essence of making you recharge and come back stronger.

- **Meditation:** When you sit alone, neglecting noises from the outside world and possible factors that bring distractions, fresh ideas find it easier to penetrate. There are different ways to meditate; you could go for yoga classes or a quiet space with like minds or yourself. This would ease your brain off a lot of stress and give room for better-thinking productivity.

- **Get an environment that soothes you:** Your definition of a soothing environment would depend on your personality type. Are you a type that likes noises, and you do better when things are happening around you? Are you the kind of individual that loves serenity, sometimes you wish everything or everyone to disappear so you can think straight? However, it is, gets yourself the right environment that would help you get a thing done at your speed.

- **Addictions:** The things you are addicted to are obvious triggers to keep you off your game. Are you the type that loves movies (when you start a series, nothing else has your attention), football, phone/social media, outings, etc.

what are those things or even people that serve as your remote control? Now you have to define everything, which brings us to the next point on the list.

- **Discipline:** A disciplined person would always have protocols and guidelines on how their day should go. How you start your morning defines how the rest of your day would go. After you have done your yearly or monthly goals and plans, map out a to-do- list, a daily schedule that would help you achieve these goals every day. No activity is too small as long as you are making things happen. Coach yourself to say no to your "addictions" encourage yourself by envisioning your results and celebrating every daily achievement.

- **Make less noise, do more:** It is okay to tell your friends about your plans and vision; in fact, this should push you to get to work. But you now have to play your part. Psychology has always proven that it is usually better to show your words via actions.

- **Don't always multitask:** You are human, after all, and multitasking isn't a bad idea at all. But how about a situation whereby you need to give your focus to a particular thing? You always cannot multitask; you would end up ruining everything and having a bad day. Some activities are technical and require your total hands and eyes. Finish one thing, then move to the other.

- **Start from the tiniest of your game:** One way to kill your zeal before you start doing any work is to see your work as one female elephant standing right in front of you. Some goals take time before they get accomplished and often serve as another discouraging factor. You would, therefore, begin to feel discouraged. For instance, the fact that you know you have something to do brings this "unrest" in your mind. How about seeing it as a hobby rather than a duty? It all depends on your mindset. See every activity as the tiniest.

- **You cannot do it all:** There comes to a point where you have to be realistic to yourself. If you feel you cannot, then drop it after you have tried. You can always skip it and then face easier ones. If you wish, you can go back to it. Don't be lazy; instead, be real with yourself.

- **Carry out your tasks immediately:** Ideas fly, energies vanish. Get your jobs done immediately. Psychology has proved this to us over and over again. Whenever an idea pops in your head for some minutes and is not backed up with actions, it tends to sour, and your will power would be tampered with. So act on them immediately, don't let them linger for more than five seconds.

- **Adequate planning:** Don't overload yourself with tasks; you are not a robot. Have you ever tasked yourself to get about five tasks done within a day? How was the outcome? You would find out that the zeal is usually there whenever you are putting yourself to this task, but the problem arises when it is time to fulfill them. How come? This is because the tasks were too much for you to handle and not realistic enough. And you most times end up doing nothing because you were too overwhelmed with the things you have to get done. With time, you would become an expert, but if you feel or think three tasks are what you can handle, kindly go ahead. Buy yourself a drink after you tick those tasks "done" in your diary.

In conclusion, though these obstacles exist, they can be managed appropriately. There are various possible ways this can be achieved if you are ready.

Chapter 21: Stay on the Road Without Distractions

Catherine Pulsifer defined focus as a means of eliminating distractions, not just from other people but also from the things we do to distract ourselves. It is not alien to humans than in the sphere of life, and one needs to focus on executing a goal, target, and get things done intentionally. We cannot talk about staying on the road without distraction, and focus won't come to mind. Many dreams won't be fulfilled, and visions won't see the light of the day, goals will be unmet because many people won't be able to pay the price of eliminating distractions within and without. You can have an awesome plan and out of this world purpose; if you lack focus, you have nothing.

Focus is a five-letter word that makes any individual ignite their potential to execute a plan, making them great. It can make a man leave a golden footprint on the sands of time and season. Life is the center of mass distraction. In as much as you are sojourning in it, distraction will come. Distraction is for the living and not the dead; one you are a living thing, be ready to be distracted. Distraction coming your way is not the problem; managing and eliminating it should be your concern. Though you need to know there is some distraction you attract to yourself because you are without a goal, the cure for this is to search for your purpose. The distraction you need to eliminate here is for those who have to find their purpose, have a goal, and are ready to achieve it.

Distractions come from within and without and are caused by internal and external factors. From within, it can be doubt, low self-esteem, ignorance, and fear from without, economic and environmental factors. Whichever way it is, it can be overcome by being focused. Distraction is also segmented into three types:

1. **Visual:** This is based on what you can see. The economy and environmental factors sponsor this, over-worrying about the nation's state, about what you will achieve in the next five years with the country's situation instead of taking it one step at a time. What we see is good and what we choose to see is better, or else, we will never get anything done.

2. **Manual**: This type of distraction deals with what we have done so far. This can be explained in two ways, and they are two extremes. A Christian hymn will say, "count your blessings," which is wise but don't count your blessings and stop trying because you are disappointed, and don't count your blessing and stop growing because you think you have arrived. Don't let what you have and what you don't have to be a stumbling block for you.

3. **Cognitive:** Both manual and visual distractions are contributors to cognitive distraction. It is a distraction from within, of the mind, a product of what we have seen, heard, and handled. This kind of distraction is the one that produces fear, doubt, low self-esteem, and many other negative mindsets.

As said earlier, being focused is the comprehensive system by which distractions can be avoided and eliminated as we strive to stay on the road.

Characteristics of Being Focused

I once read the story of a young boy on the internet, of about eight years old that walked up to the General Commandment of the Army of a country, and he told the General, "I want to be like you when I grow up." The General looked at him and smiled. I believe he must wonder why a small boy would want to grow up and become a leader in the military. They stared at the young man and asked him all over again, *"Are you sure you want to be like me when you grow up?"*

The boy affirmatively said, *"Yes."*

The General then replied to the boy with the most heartless answer anyone can give a little boy. He said, *"Take a glass of water and walk around this field."*

That must have been a simple assignment; who cannot walk around a field with a cup? That must have been my thought if I were the boy.

But the General said more, *"The cup will be filled to the brim, and not a drop of water must splash on the floor. Well, if it does, I will order the soldiers to shoot you."*

Wow, if I were the boy, I would have dropped the cup and run away. But, he did not. The boy agreed and started the journey.

Every step the boy took, there were distractions around him. Ladies were dancing around him on the left, other children of his age playing ball, and the Army parading, but he never stopped.

What a focused heart?

The boy never stopped, he kept moving, and finally, he arrived back at the General's feet, and guess what the General said to him.

"You have done well for yourself, and you can become a General someday."

Imagine if you were the boy? Would you have remained determined?

Being focused has its set of characteristics, and it is these attributes that make it possible to journey without distractions.

1. **Learning:** A focused mind is one that is always ready to learn and flexible to change. Ignorance is a distraction, a popular one, and it takes knowledge to cure it. You can not be focused without learning; you can not be focused if you are willing to let go of practices that bring you distractions no matter how awesome they may be. One of the greatest abilities of men who have remained steadfast on the road is learning—men like Nelson Mandela and Winston Churchill.

2. **Courage:** Knowledge, confidence, courage itself aid you in overcoming fear. Fear is a kind of distraction; courage is its cure. Being courageous emboldened your mind, and in the process, makes you focus. Courage is needed to conquer doubt. If doubt is conquered, fear won't have an environment to grow.

3. **Consistency:** Getting a focus is not magic though it looks like one after you might have completed the process. Learning and being courageous doesn't end; it is a daily operation, which calls for continuous practice. Consistency is a top-notch attribute if you get things done and stay on the road without distractions. The need to continue even when it doesn't make sense imprints our set

goal on our mind until we achieve it. Consistency is the spirit of a focused mind.

4. **Resilience:** Doggedness, ruggedness, it is like the hardness of a soldier, which is always endured no matter what comes their way. Nothing good comes easy, and this true. To be focused is sweet to the mouth but bitter to the belly, but if you pay the price early, it will save you from the wind of distraction that will try to push you off the road to success. Being focused is hard work; it is the violence staying by force, which calls for the need to be resilient and positively stubborn.

5. **Know yourself:** You are a lion, don't behave like a sheep. Activate your strengths and work on your weaknesses. Become your best; come out of that shell. Know your identity, and you are born to succeed; you have your place in life. If need be, get an excellent daily confession devotional and speak to yourself. Your words carry power and believe absolutely in the good, and you can do no matter the bad that has come from you in the past. You are not a failure, never. This is the best way to overcome self-esteem issues and inferiority complexes, which are distractions from the mind.

The challenge of distractions has been dissected, and solutions have been proffered. Staying on the road without distractions is now easier; you need to get the job done by working on the characteristics of being focused day by day till it is wrought in you. Continue to say focus.

Chapter 22: Principles of Time Management

"Most of us spend too much time on what is urgent and little time on what is important."

- Steven Covey

Steve's quote captured what I envisioned when it comes to the subject of time management. Merriam Webster dictionary defined time as the measured or measurable period during which an action, process, or condition exists or continues. In contrast, management is the act or skill of controlling and making decisions about a business or a goal. Time management is the act of controlling and making decisions within a measurable period during which the action continues. Time management is a skill any man who will get things done at the right time must-have. It doesn't come by wishing, but by practice.

Time management is the process of exercising consciousness over how you spend your time and planning to increase effectiveness, efficiency, and productivity. Time management is a conscious effort, a process, and it has a goal. Time management is essential for man's development in every area of life. A famous saying goes, "Time is money," which shows the worth of time. Time is expensive; how we use our time goes a long way in determining how we will manage our lives. Time is worth more than rubies. We have more than one way of tackling time management. You can get self-help books, download apps, adjust your schedule, make to-do lists, etc. But if you haven't come to an understanding of why you need to manage your time, it will be futile. If you don't have the knowledge to use them, you can't. I will be explaining some reasons why it is important to manage your time effectively. The benefits of time management:

- **Creating a conducive environment for effectiveness:** until some people start learning to manage their time, they won't know the beauty and see the need to create a personal cubicle for yourself. You can sometimes achieve in the crowd no matter how much you try to fit in, and they will drag you back, especially if what you are involved in is a personal project and not a group project. Just imagine a high school without a stipulated resumption and closing hour; their level of disorganization would be terrible. Time management would help you to be effective through creating a conducive environment. Know when to tell people you are busy; you can't afford to be distracted.

- **The setting of priorities:** One of the greatest lights in time management is, "Don't allow any man to set your priorities for you; you set it by yourself." No man can set your priorities better than you do; I understand we now have professionals in this field of setting priorities, but it is still expedient that every priority set is almost a hundred about you. Your purpose, passion, and goals should be useful here; you set priorities according to them. Your priorities can be divided into urgent and important and how much you can sort these things with balance. Know that urgent is different from important. A goal may be urgent and not important, but when it is important, it is urgent. Know what you can do on your own, what you need help on, and what you need to pay to acquire. Setting priorities makes you consistent and spares you from distractions on the road. You should know when to keep your phone away or switch it off, or set the alarm. Time management will teach a lot, ranging from how to manage your time to achieve your goals under a short period because you will be compelled to do away with issues or people, which I will call "time wasters."

- **The reduction of time spent on non-priorities:** There is an activity we do or is involved in that won't contribute any value to our lives. It is good for people to catch fun and hang out with friends but don't do it to the detriment of your success. You can vividly reduce the time allocated to some activities and reject some. Reduction in time spent on non-priorities will increase your time management skill and make you better overall. When you are willing to manage your time, reduce the time you spend on important things.

- **Implementation of goals**: Success is a man action film with different characters. If you don't act your cast with a mindset of implementing and achieving your goals, you will spend forever at a spot. Implementation of goals is an important factor in time management. Having goals will compel you to set a period for its execution, and it will drive you to make a timetable. This may look simple and basic, but your consistency in doing this will transform your mind into adapting to the consciousness of "time wait for no man."

- **Reduce stress:** There is this possibility of being drained of every pinch of energy by doing less important things. Your ability to manage time will help you to reduce stress. Doing the right thing at the right time will make you escape the burdens and challenges that come with loads of work. Are you getting stressed after work daily? Managing time will help you meet deadlines; I don't think there is another kind of pressure draining that a man undergoes when a deadline needs to be met. It is better to estimate how long a given task will take you to complete, and you know you can meet the deadline with reduced stress.

- **Self-discipline:** Self-discipline is valuable when you adhere to good time management. It doesn't allow procrastination. The better you perform, the more your self-discipline. You will get to a point where you become your self-prosecutor, especially when you do not live within the functionality of your present and future goals plans.

"You can't make up for wasted time, but you can achieve better in the future." Ashley Ormon, author

Every benefit of time management improves all other facets of your life. You need to start learning how to manage your time or the principles of time management.

- **Planning:** Planning is important in whatever you do. In the morning or stipulated time, take a few minutes to plan your activities for the day, week, or month. Get a diary (soft or hard copy) and jot down your activities; this will help you minimize distractions. Review your activities or planning daily or according to your plan layout. Don't go out without it. Make a list of your priorities in the diary and act by it. Find a time to quickly address or make a mental calculation of the list of things to be done until your goals are achieved.

- **The 80/20 Rule:** This rule is also referred to as the Pareto's Principle when applied to work, which means that approx. twenty percent of your hard work produces 80 percent results. So, you should focus that 20 percent on making the most effective use of your time.

- **Step by step:** Avoid working under pressure, trying to do many things at a time – don't try to do it all at once. Don't put undue pressure on yourself when you don't need pressure at all. If you want to write, write if you're going to type, type. Some processes need you to do one thing at a time, don't multitask, or else it reduces your efficiency and level of concentration.

- **Organize:** You cannot be organized if you don't prioritize. You have to know what is urgent and what is important and tackle it after the order depending on their time intervals and deadline. This will help you to know the urgent and the important.

- **Delegate:** No one man can do it all; delegate some of your tasks to others, as much as they have the necessary knowledge and skills to execute the task.

Whether you have started to manage your time or become a professional in time management skills, striving to benefit from the principles will surely aid your greatness.

Chapter 23: Develop the Spartan's Self-Discipline

"Discipline is the soul of a strict man – army. Discipline makes small numbers formidable, and procures success to the esteem, and the weak respectively."

– George Washington.

It must first be established that self-discipline comes with personal effort via a painful process. A round peg cannot fit a square hole; it will need to be remodified for use and purpose. Wishes are fantasies, but self-discipline is a horse you ride on your way to greatness. Others can not do it for you, and you cannot avoid it or buy it; you can only do it by yourself. The only set of people who don't see self-discipline as a needful skill don't have direction. Self-discipline is one ability and capacity, a determining factor to depth in life. It takes it to search and find purpose, stay on the road without distraction, manage time, and build one's stress relief.

The importance of self-discipline is becoming clearer than before, if not more so. Discipline brings freedom to us, empowers us to pursue that which we truly desire—achieving our goals and attaining a remarkable and purposeful life. However, the absence of self-discipline makes us submit to the wind of distraction. You must be prepared to pay the price of self-discipline, which can be painful. But as Jim Rohn said, *"We must all suffer one of two things: we either suffer the pain of regret, or we suffer the pain of discipline."*

Self-discipline is the secret to success because the principle of success cannot be useful without self-discipline. It prepares you for the opportunity, and it is the strength of the weak.

Dominic Mann, in his book Spartan Discipline, said, *"In ancient Greece, it was widely accepted that a single Spartan warrior was worth at least three or four non-Spartan soldiers. The discipline of the Spartans was so legendary that they evoked the admiration of even their enemies."* A man cannot be strong beyond his self-discipline level, as shown in the Spartan soldiers' way of life and quality. It is no news that the training soldiers undergo is strict and tough; no man passes through the system and becomes *"normal"* again. The training is to beat them into the mold of one who can defend her nation and the people anyhow and anywhere. But even at the level of their training, there is a testimony made concerning the Spartan warriors, which are heart-catching. It was even widely accepted by their enemies, and they were worth three or four times better than themselves. It wasn't the survival of the fittest war, and the fittest were distinct and well defined.

The Spartan warriors were admired by their enemy made me remember a saying about being diligent in the Christian book. It says, *"If you are diligent, your gift will make you stand before kings."* I am sure the Spartans' legends would have made them stand before countless kings and leave many men in awe of their gift. The fittest is not physically strong; the fittest is he or she whose mind is steadfast in self-discipline. Self-discipline makes you triumph and become better than the best. If you desire to be successful in your choosing field of endeavor, it is needed. As earlier stipulated, its process is painful, which is true, but the better news is, it will not take too long. Once you have mastered the act of discipline, you will find joy and peace doing it.

1. **Spartan minimalism:** This is an act that involves the increase of focus by the elimination of distractions. As Bruce Lee said, *"A successful warrior is an average man, with laser-like focus."* This is not hard, though; it is all about perspectives; somebody who doesn't have junk or other food with high calories won't need to worry about unnecessarily adding weight. Somebody without a phone won't need to bother about owning a charger. This is also applicable to you, and you won't need to avoid issues that distract you if you have eliminated them in the first place. This is dealing with the root, not the leaves. One of the foundations upon which the Spartans' discipline rests is their philosophy of simplicity over decoration and

precision over expansiveness. Many well-known men like Mark Zuckerberg of Facebook adopt this way of life. Mark wears the same shirt every day, and he believes wearing the same shirt daily helps him focus on his dream. And truly, he pays attention to how to serve his community (Facebook) better. Eliminate everything that is not aligned with your goals or purpose and see you soar beyond your wildest imagination.

1. **Be Tough:** One of the greatest assets the Spartans soldiers had is their hunger; they create hunger after every successful battle. There is a kind of vigor a man on an empty stomach fights for food; he fights with his all, and he doesn't mind if he does but will do everything to stay alive and eat. This is the kind of toughness you need, like a man who has no other option. The day you start having a plan B over what a plan A can achieve shows your lack of self-discipline, and you won't become your best in such ways.

2. **Rule your mind:** "Rule your mind, or it will rule you." — Buddha. The Western religion or the monks has this special ability to meditate for an extended period, which gives them the capacity to rule their minds. Your motto should be mind over matter because your body can withstand anything, but your mind has to convince it that it can. If you lose the battle in your mind, your body is

useless. Sometimes you feel that you can't do more again, and you want to relent; it is an indication that you have more strength to do more. Once you can rule your mind, it will. The ability to rule your mind cannot be achieved in a day; hence you need to practice continually. Muhammad Ali says, *"When it comes to self-discipline, mind over matter."*

3. **Be rigid:** This means be rugged, be resilient, and don't give up. The toughness of a process and the seemingly low result should not make you stop doing the right things that would make you a better person. Your willpower should be unchanging and unbending; close your heart to forces of discouragement. Even when external factors want to usurp your process, let your heart be hard as a diamond, let it become impenetrable in as much that it will destroy your motivation.

4. **The two types of want:** The want of the body and the need of the mind. The body wants to crave distractions that need to be eliminated and don't yield to it. The need of the mind is what is needed for you to be better and become the best. Your mind should always control your body as it is your mind that you have trained; it takes time before the body align. Don't yield to the pressure your body is putting on your mind, and it is not as powerful as your mind; your mind should conquer your body's desire.

5. **No excuse:** This is the easiest way to be defeated, trying to defend yourself when there is a setback. Don't forget you are in charge, don't try to exonerate yourself, accept defeat and rebuke and fire again. Let this be in you, no excuse for lack of hunger, no excuse for not ruling your mind, no excuse for not putting your body under, no excuse for not practicing simplicity and eliminating distractions, no excuse for not having been tough, for not having been rigid. No excuse for not attaining the highest level of self-discipline, no excuse for not becoming better than the present.

Having known all these, remember discipline is your soul, your pathway to greatness, embrace it.

Chapter 24: Build Your Stress-Relief

*"It is not the stress we face that kills us, it is our reaction to stress that does" - **Hans Selye***

Stress is emotional or physical coercion that people experience. It can be born from any action or thought that makes you feel frustrated, angry, or nervous. Stress is a weighty feeling that affects the mind and the body; it leaves the mind clumsy and heavy. There is a little amount of stress that is needed and useful when it is for meeting a target or beating a deadline. You may need to make yourself uncomfortable for a short time to get things down. But when stress is elongated in engagement affairs, and we fail to control it, it is hazardous. Your body releases hormones as a way of reacting to stress; these hormones make your brain cautious, put your muscles under pressure, and increase your heartbeat. Stress is not a disease, not a sickness, but its victims' carelessness waters their seed.

There are two types of stress: **acute and chronic stress**. Acute is a positive kind of stress which makes you excited and brings an ecstasy-like feeling to your body. Chronic kinds of stress can cause different diseases, which can display other emotional and physical symptoms. In some cases, you may not know why you feel sick and tired is because of stress. Here are examples of illness and symptoms that may indicate that you are stressed:

- Constipation

- Diarrhea

- Headaches

- Tiredness

- Sexual problems

- Forgetfulness

- Lack of energy

- Insomnia

- Weight loss or gain

- Upset stomach

- Frequent pains

In 2017, we lost a darling lecturer in our department to the grave. The last time I saw him, he was beaming with smiles and full of life. It was shocking to hear he died after he slumped and rushed to the nearest clinic. Stress was said to be the major factor that ruined his health. It is easier to understand his being under the canopy of stress because of his commitment and workload. Shockingly, someone as exposed as he could be ignorant of his health status and fail to keep himself under control. We lost him to ignorance and lackadaisical disposition; stress did not kill him, but his reaction did. Masking emotional or body stress with a smile and more workload will cut short one's longevity. I see people who overstress themselves in this light, *"they don't value their life."*

Ignorance and lackadaisical attitude are the two major factors why people are consumed with stress and lose their lives. Ignorance is also a fuel that fuels the fire of self-destruction. But this is an information age, a time when you can visit the internet to check out diseases attached to suspected symptoms; no man should be in the darkness of stress and its negative effects. I want to believe anybody who does due to stress happens to take it lightly. There is a need to know when stress becomes chronic, its accompanying symptoms, its numerous side effects, control it, and how to build stress relief.

1. **Meditate:** Research suggests that daily meditation may alter the brain's neural pathways, making you more resilient to stress," says psychologist Robbie Maller Hartman, Ph.D., a Chicago health and wellness coach. Meditation is not worrying or thinking, and people make this mistake a lot. When you are still thinking about how bad your day is, how you don't have what to eat tomorrow or how your wife has been nagging you, you are not

meditating. Stop worrying over what worry can not solve; worrying is an unnecessary weight in your heart.

Free your mind by allowing your heart to see beyond your present predicament, let your imagination be that of joy and fulfillment, and let it continue for 30 to 45 minutes. Your body will be free from heaviness and mind from clumsiness. Practice this in a silent and serene environment.

2. **Deep breathing:** Deep breathing counters the effects of stress by slowing the heart rate and lowering blood pressure," psychologist Judith Tutin says. When you have your heart racing, maybe because you ran hard or had a sudden, shocking experience or a stressful week, it indicates stress. Such experiences always make people lose consciousness and the heart pump hard, abnormally. The best approach is to take a deep breath for 30 seconds or one minute and release the air. Do this continuously till your heartbeat is normalized.

3. **Reach out:** Hanging out with friends who make you smile and relieve you of worries or labor is important. You can call people with a listening ear who won't crucify you to pour out that stresses your mind. A problem shared is a stress solution. Taking a break to retreat is a great idea and use that opportunity to relax and save yourself from things

that distract you, finding a new way to make you effective without accumulating stress.

4. **Laugh out loud:** Normalize laughing and smiling, laugh or smile out of the blue; nobody has to inspire it. When you remember, you have to laugh, laugh. Watch comedy skit if need be, read humor-laced articles and stay around people who make you laugh a lot. Laughing even makes you look radiant, and note that it is not to cover-up stress but to relieve you of stress.

5. **Gratitude:** One of the important things that should be precious to a man that we don't value is gratitude. We lose our sense of gratitude because we did not count it; we only focus on what we don't have. What we don't have is the main reason why we stress our minds and body. Get a gratitude diary, take a record of every good thing that happens to you through the day, week, and month. They will serve as a source of hope for you when things become tough and challenging. Being positive also aids your sense of being grateful even for things you don't attach importance to. It is massive and straightforward stress relief.

6. **Eat:** It is astonishing how people use their bodies without having a good and balanced meal. An efficient engine without good oiling will damage it. Don't skip food; some

people are calm about this. They can work the whole day without eating, which can ruin the long run's body system. Food, good food, can relieve you of stress. Don't wait till you slump at the alarm to eat if you are easily immersed in what you are doing. Eat fruits also, and its vitamins can help to flourish the brain. Don't take too much junk also.

7. **Sleep:** Sleeping is not lying on a bed and closing your eyes. Sleeping is a long rest. One of the beauties of sleeping is undue pressure is shaken off. The nerves relax, the heart regularly beats, and body joints are at ease. If you know you won't sleep at night because you will be busy, find time to sleep if not even more than two hours during the day and vice versa. Nothing can take the place of sleeping than sleeping. Know the kind of setting where you sleep, and stay put. Before you sleep, let having a water bath be a lifestyle. There is a kind of refreshment that comes with it and an effect it gives to the mind and the body.

Building your stress relief is important for anybody who loves their lives, who want to enjoy the dividend of their labor. Stress cannot cause singlehandedly wreck a man, and it needs the permission of the man. Your stress reaction will determine if you will mar it, or it will mar you. You only live once, make it stress-free.

Chapter 25: Respect Your Commitments to Others and Yourself

Regardless of what you like or hate, you are committed to one thing or the other. Every human is essentially committed to eating, brushing their teeth, and bathing; married couples are committed to each other, and students are committed to their books. This simply means that we are all committed to one thing or the other because; we want to see a particular desired result, we want to make things happen, we want to see certain changes in specific areas of our lives. With all of these being said, commitment simply has to do with being dedicated to a particular activity or cause.

The Power of Commitment

Being dedicated to something or someone is so strong that it influences how you think, the things you do and how you live generally. Commitment to something or someone is more like a compass that directs your life, and it shows you the path in which you must walk if you want to make things work. Commitment is so strong that it possesses the lifetime of an individual. For instance, every human commits to belief and their philosophy of life; this then controls everything we do in life.

Tips to Help You Respect Your Commitment to Yourself

Note that you cannot respect your commitment to another person if you have not first admired the dedication you have for yourself. The old saying goes that "You cannot give what you do not have." One factor that helps you keep the commitment to yourself is called "Self-respect" the quality of your life is dependent on how well you treat yourself and how you allow others to treat you. Self-respect gives you a level of self-confidence; it makes you believe that all your goals are achievable. It brings about positive feelings and good emotions about yourself.

Here are some factors that could help improve your self-respect:

- **Choose to respect yourself:** choosing to respect yourself is a commitment. Do a heart check of ways you have disrespected yourself and the things you should stop doing. For instance, have you been too available for some people? Have you stayed off issues that you should stay off? Are you still putting up with some people or relationships? You think about these and keep choosing self-respect every day.

- **Affirm that you deserve the best treatment and act likewise:** Are you the time that tends to sulk in emotions? You take all the insults from people because you do feel you want peace? Then it is time to see things from another angle. The way you see yourself would determine the way others would treat you. Affirm that you deserve to be treated with care and kindness because you would do so to others. Be bold enough to stand up to anyone who would overstep their boundaries. Set self-rules and stick to them. There is a common statement that respect is reciprocal, so ensure that you accord people respect in the same measure you want or desire to be respected.

- **Always consider how you feel:** your emotions are essential, and they deserve your full attention. Don't bottle them. Study yourself; what actions or words make you uncomfortable? Take time to study your emotions and act on them.

- **Pay attention to your emotional needs:** what are your emotional needs? What are the things that make you happy when you feel emotionally down? It could be that you need to let go of some toxic relationships, people who always make you feel less of yourself. Another issue is that you may tend to depend on people to make you feel a certain way. This is where disrespect for yourself sets in.

Take time to study your emotional needs and find ways to meet them. Respect yourself.

Tips to Help You Keep Your Commitment to Others

- **Create a list in your journal:** staying dedicated to a cause is a conscious choice; that is, you remind yourself to live by this choice of yours every day. As you pick up your pen and journal, ask yourself these questions; who are the VIPs in my life? What should I be committed to achieving these goals? For instance, if you are on the fat side and you want to lose weight, there are some things you should be committed to, such as the doctor's advice, exercise, fasting, etc. so, sincerely write them out.

- **Give room for people:** How do people feel around you? Do they feel judged? What atmosphere or aura do you give? Give them a chance to express themselves, give listening ears, encourage those around you, and give the love you can.

- **Consistency:** One key factor to genuine commitment is consistency. You will be like a double-minded person or an unserious person if you are not consistent with your commitment. Commitment and consistency go hand in hand. If you would be committed to something, there has to be consistency if you want to get results. Lack of consistency has a hand in the failed attempt of everyone who has ever tried to be committed to one thing or the other.

- **Be committed to yourself:** Commitment to others starts with being committed to yourself and taking yourself seriously. Be obsessed about making things work and staying true to who or what you believe in.

- **Wisely create your scale of preference:** Everyone has a goal or objective they seek to achieve within a stipulated period; you and I are not exempted. However, according to their level of importance in your life, there is a need to grade these things. Think of your life goals, the things worth committing to, the most paramount things to achieve these goals.

- **Record your successes and encourage yourself:** One of the hardest things to do in life is coping with fellow humans, especially in scenarios where you are putting all your strength to make things work. The other party seems to be taking you for granted. Learn to manage people, give them the respect they deserve, but if they are not worth it after your efforts, you can always walk away. List out the people or things you are committed to and how consistent you have been, and how things have been working because of your conscious efforts.

Benefits of Committing to Yourself and Others

Commitment is an indication of your existence, and it means that you are living and that you are making progress. There is hardly anyone living without being committed to something or someone. Some benefits of commitment include;

- **Self-respect and integrity:** Commitment helps you to understand respecting yourself fully. It enables you to figure out your feelings, the things that hurt you, and what makes you happy.

- **Fulfillment**: It helps you achieve personal and collective goals. It could be in your organization, your social groups, and even among your peers.

- **Love and respect for others:** When you choose to commit yourself to something or someone, it means that you have a certain form of respect and love for them. In other words, commitment brings about rapid increment in your love and respect for other people.

- **Discipline:** Certain factors trigger self-discipline, and commitment is one of them. You just feel like doing certain things, but you remind yourself of the things or people you have decided to stay true to. This then brings in you the ability to discipline yourself.

- **Growth:** As you begin to see the need to be accountable to yourself and others, growth automatically sets it.

In conclusion, commitment is a choice and no action that should be done out of compulsion. A huge sign of a sense of responsibility is consistent in who or whatever you have chosen to give your commitment. Respect commitment to yourself first, and then pass it on to others.

Chapter 26: Proactivity vs. Positive Thinking

"I believe that everyone can choose how to approach life. So, if you are a proactive individual, you should focus on preparing. If you are a reactive individual, you should focus on repairing."
— *John C. Maxwell*

All fingers are not equal is a common and handy quote for humans because it is a fact, and experiencing it is easy. The inequality of fingers is also applicable when we want to discuss the class where an individual belongs. Normally, people are distributed to the lower class, middle class, and upper class depending on their economic and financial power. Nobody chooses this, but this is the place they find themselves, maybe good or bad. But there is one factor that brings men of different classes to the same level: the *"the power of choice."* You may be poor and choose to be poor forever; that is your choice. The same thing for the rich; they choose to become poor; it all depends on the right things they do and the wrong things they avoid. This is not the major point here, but the ability is made to see the importance of the power of choice that every man possesses. Proactivity and positive thinking are popular thoughts from popular men, they are weapons used to fight battles on their way to greatness, and they prescribe it to their mentees or protégés also. Though positive thinking seems to be more popular, does that mean it is more potent than proactivity, which can also be considered proactive thinking?

Proactivity is the act of controlling a situation by making things happen or preparing for possible future problems. Still, positive thinking often leads one to accept what is happening and suffer the events passively. Instead, the proactive thinker uses resilience to break out of the current paradigm and find the opportunity behind what others see as a defeat and creates a wonderful new reality. Proactive thinking focuses on preparing, while positive thinking focuses on repairing. Positive thinkers are, most of the time, people who come up with a lot of ideas but don't focus on acting on any of the ideas. Positive thinking makes you look like it, but you will not become it because you won't act. You need to practice proactive thinking effectively, and it will aid you in procuring, increasing your willpower, and strengthening your self-discipline.

There are three types of people when it comes to setting a goal and achieving it. Some make things happen, those who watch what happens, and those who wonder what happened. Those who make things happen are those who embrace productivity. Philosophers believe we all have the ability and capacity as humans to become the kind of person that makes things happen. This means all men can reflect the proactive attribute if they have enough inspiration to propel them in any circumstances. Several benefits come with proactivity.

1. **Saves time and money:** This doesn't mean you won't spend money, or it won't require time; instead, it implies preparation saves you from unplanned spending and unforeseen circumstances. When you plan, you won't need to be doing crash courses or looking for impromptu solutions to avoidable problems.

2. **Prepare you for situations**: It is like having a backup plan if things did not go the way you were prepared, and an avoidance event just occurred, which demands immediate reaction from you. But how do you attend to a challenge you don't prepare for when you did not prepare for a situation you were supposed to prepare for? When you are preparing, it is easy to foresee like a scientist what are the familiar barriers that will make your effort unfruitful. A person who wants to organize an open-air program will be proactive enough to acquire or rent a tent.

3. **Recognize a need for change:** Being proactive means being sincere. You are not trying to make a funny mental note and avoid the reality of unfruitfulness attached to what you are doing at hand. Being proactive will make you discover the flaws in your sky and impurities in your gold. It makes you cut the needful and do away with the

unnecessary right away. You don't manage when you are proactive, it's either you don't use it or find a lasting solution.

4. **Improves creativity:** You won't know how innovative proactivity can be until you get to a stage in your life when you can't do without it. Your creativity increases, and you start getting new ways of getting things done. This is when you will discover more than one answer to a question; this is when you will see the beauty of being proactive. This is when you will learn how to think out of the box. As a budding writer, I find it hard to write when there is no inspiration, and this can go on for more than a month, but when I became a professional, and I see the need to meet up with deadlines, I have to devise a means of meeting up by proactivity. Not until then, I never knew some things are achievable, which led to unlearning a lot of old habits. Proactivity will increase your curiosity level.

5. **Flexible:** You can't be proactive and be rigid; it is impossible. Because being proactive will make you break through familiar barriers and dig new wells of ideas beyond what you have always known. You will have many options and find suitable properties that suit each. It makes you look beyond the present and look into the future.

6. **Peace:** Once you have self-confidence, you will start experiencing peace. There will be little or nothing to fear of things not working out because you have been able to foresee any facts that may come up through proactivity.

7. **Clear direction for the future:** Proactivity will make you define your future because you start planning early, not like many who use the quote *"what will be will be."* It will enable you to do the right things at the right time because you know where you are going. There is no person whose figure is as clear as the man who knows his future and knows how to get there.

8. **Self-improvement:** The fear of failure will disappear when you are proactive. Because you don't have any choice but to act, sometimes our lack of preparation makes us fear failing. You will start getting things done intentionally, and your little and big victories will be a painkiller to your numerous failures.

Being proactive has some benefits instead of positive thinking. Below is the nature of proactivity.

- **It is anticipatory:** It involves showing up before any problems occur, instead of some wishful thinking, just like my mother showed her friend concerning the need or a house before the problem becomes big.

- **It is change-oriented**: Being proactive means taking over and making things happen instead of waiting for an eternity for a change that will never occur. One of the problems many underdeveloped countries in Africa are facing is our inability to be proactive.

- **It is self-initiated**: This can be achieved personally; the individual just needs to have a conviction and see the importance of going for it. The individual does not need to be asked to act, nor do they require detailed instructions. For example, though the woman required a work of inspiration from my mother, she was the one who initiated and executed it.

The need for proactivity cannot be overemphasized; embrace it.

Chapter 27: Motivation Is Bullshit (or: The Motivation Trap)

Do you always want motivation to work and get started with your goals? Are you always struggling to keep to your goals without having some incentives to motivate you? Do you think you cannot achieve anything without someone constantly motivating you? If yes, I am pleased to tell you that you are in the motivation trap. What is the motivation trap, and why are you trapped in it?

Motivation is a great tool to help you stand firm and consistent, but when you cannot take any cations, make progress in your life without you having anyone to motivate, it is evident you are in a motivation trap.

Motivation is crappy, and you read that, right?

I believe that a mind with a burning desire does not need anyone to motivate or fuel it. How did you prepare for your exams as a College student? Did you wait for some people to encourage you? Did you want someone to inspire you to read? Did you wait for someone to organize three days webinar to help you find the right desire to read? If not, then why do you have to wait for some motivation to make the right choice?

When you know what you want, you do not need to invest in some motivational speeches to tell you some stories that you can do it. You need to be able to motivate yourself by yourself.

What are your dreams? What is your ambition? Do you sleep each night, remembering those dreams? Do you wake up with the desire to achieve your dreams? If you did any of those, then you are on the right track.

Get out of that motivational trap.

Don't be deluded into thinking that you cannot take action yourself. It is a big delusion that has trapped many people's dreams. Don't be in that league. You can know what you want. If you can do it, then you don't need some extra motivation. This may be a bitter pill to swallow, but trust me, it is the truth. Most times, motivations are meant for babies; if you are a parent, you know how much time you spend motivating your son or daughter to sip a teacup when they are ill or does their assignment to play games with their friends. You are not a baby, and you are an adult. You are a business owner, an employee, an entrepreneur, and many more; you should not wait for some motivational stories.

How to Avoid Being the Motivation Trap

Many people do not know about motivation because it is unreliable and inconsistent. Will your boss always be in a good move to motivate you every morning? Will your partner always be available to provide you with incentives? Will your friends always be interested in inspiring you with some exciting words? Motivation brings excitement, and sometimes excitement does not last forever. Just like dopamine raises your emotions, motivations raise your excitement level; however, they are bound to expire if the motivation is not within. As much as you need someone to inspire you from outside, ensure that you always motivate yourself to do the right thing at all times. Here are a few ways to avoid the motivation trap:

Know What You Desire, and Stick to It

Many times, people make the mistake of not knowing what they want. I have realized that people who don't know what they want or have a clear purpose in life are always excited about different things. Two men went to see a life coach; the first person is named Jack, while the second man is named Williams. Jack desires to be a human rights lawyer, and he loves fighting for the weak and poor in society; the only problem he has is he doesn't know if that will be the best move for him since he has great records with political law.

On the other hand, Williams is a graduate of law, doesn't know what he wants, or is heading. Although he is currently working at a law firm, he has no goal or future ambition aside from his job, which is not sure if the law is meant for him.

Williams and Jack are both in need of clarity and answers. They both have questions. They both walk into the office of a life coach, who shared several stories of great men in the world today. The life coach ended the coaching session with the following words, *"Your dreams are valid and big. Don't stop dreaming and taking the right actions for your dream."* These words acted differently in the minds of these two men.

Jack kept pondering those words and never stopped until he launched his first project to deal with human trafficking and racial discrimination. At the same time, Williams is still struggling to achieve results effectively. Funnily enough, Williams was so excited as soon as he heard the stories of these successful men, despite his excitement, he could not take any reasonable action. Many people like Williams today get excited in the face of motivation and slack immediately; the excitement is over. The slack is not farfetched because these people who often slack do not know what they want. Some of them are simply following the crowd.

Find Your Place

The moment you know what you want, the next thing to do is to find your place. Where do you belong? What do you see? Who are the people in your class and categories?

The bitter truth about the fact remains that not all place is yours to fill. If you desire to be a singer and are clergy, you may need to be motivated to perform your duties as a clergy. Many people find their jobs boring because they are not doing what they want or they have lost their passion for the job. There is a place for you; find it. Even in your workplace, there is a position for you. Just do your part by seeing it and ensuring that you know what suits you best.

Do It Now

Time cannot wait for anyone, but the irony is that we can wait for the right time. Have you ever tried to tell the time to slow down a bit for you because you late for an interview? If you experienced that, then you need to be like Nike, "Just do it," and need I say that the reason you are taking action is that it is a necessity. Taking actions at the right time is very important. If you need to get out of your bed to work remotely, a dear friend does it. One of the things I do is that I allow my dreams to wake me up. I allow the goals that I have not achieved to chase me out of bed. I always tell myself I cannot rest until I have achieved my dreams.

Invest in Your Habits

Habits are highly important, and there are certain habits that you must invest in. Reading books, investing in knowledge, going to bed early, and every other form of healthy habits are essential in life. There are no hacks to great productivity, but you can improve your habits to achieve results.

Prioritize Your Skills and Tasks

How do you handle your tasks? I have realized that some people have problems multitasking; hence they have to wait until they are entirely done with a particular task. You need to find out what you love to do and how you can handle the tasks. Have a scale of preference, or better still, a priority list. For instance, I write out all the things that I am determined to achieve in a day as soon as I wake up, and I prioritize them according to their importance.

Avoid Procrastination

People who procrastinate are always looking for excuses and motivation to get to work. Sometimes, these people procrastinate because they are lazy. Laziness and procrastination go hand in hand. (If you need help procrastinating, then you can read chapter 16).

Imagine the number of milestones that you must have achieved if you had not waited for motivation? I bet you would have achieved a lot. Achievements and results should not be based on motivation, and in simpler words, you should not be in motion because of what people choose to say to you or what people do not tell you. Always remember that your success is yours to start with, so guard it jealously, and ensure that you don't lose guard at all.

Chapter 28: The Magical Power Of Error

"We all make them; the difference is what we do after we make a mistake, how we see the mistake — a learning experience or a failure." - **Catherine Pulsifer**

This must be in you as it has been for every successful or great man; making basic mistakes cannot be avoided during the growth process. Whether humans like it or not, errors can't be instantly eradicated like ice on a sunny afternoon. The signs are always there; no one can deny it. It is only a dead man or an unfruitful man who will claim not to have made mistakes. Growing up, most of us, including myself, have been made to think that we will not amount to goodness when we commit an error and that we must avoid it at all costs. This may be true for some life stages, but it is impossible for a baby who wants to start walking to avoid falling. The baby will fall though the fall may differ depending on the amount of guidance and counseling available. Our citadel of learning made us feel terrible in school when we were in error, and they made us hide it like weakness in the process, making it hard for us to get better. When we do everything in deceit to avoid errors, we go from bad to worse. They never told us that the important thing to do is admit a mistake to be helped, the only way to get better. The more errors we make, the less capable we are of committing.

For others who can meet with people who are ready to help or are opportune to pass through a loving home are taught to see errors as chances to learn something new and grow. The magical power of mistakes is revealed by the learning that comes with it. Instead of avoiding them, it should be converted to opportunity the same way electrical energy is converted to thermal energy. This is what is needed to be observed through great men and women. Instead of focusing on their success, observe their process, the errors they make, and how they could come out of it.

Mistakes are not packaged in sweet experiences, so their victims are always compelled to be forever immersed in the ocean of denial and avoidance. Our past should be considered as a blessing in alignment with our present experiences. If they seem to overshadow it, we have the authority on how we choose to see it, interpret it, and allow the effect on us. More so, if the error is not our intention, whatever comes and happens after it must be our doing. You don't go into error in ignorance and come out of it, still ignorant, don't play the role of an unfruitful fool. Admitting that you are in error should not make you glory in it, should not stop you from learning from it, become better than it and grow.

Errors can come in different types like slip up, mistakes, and violation of rules. I have deduced from life experiences that three major factors are the reason for human errors. These factors will be discussed to make you not necessarily avoid them but to eliminate them before they become a thorn in your flesh. It should be noted that it is still part of the magical power of error that could help learn from other people's mistakes.

- **Ignorance:** If you fail to learn from other people's fall and rise, you will become victims of their fall and may never rise. What you don't know can ruin you. Get wisdom, get understanding, and make proper use of it. Not being ignorant won't stop you from committing some unavoidable errors, but it will save you from violating rules, making you lose your joy and make it hard for you to get it back.

- **Nonchalant attitude:** What ruined some is not what they don't know; it is what they know that they refuse to put to good use. Don't have this *"I am less concerned"* mentality, and it will only lead you to more errors. The beauty of making errors is to make you better, not to make you worse. Don't become stagnant amid error. Be willing to change.

- **Overconfidence:** What ruined Daniel in my narrated story is overconfidence; it always breeds pride. If you are not humble in the face of error, refusing to justify yourself and shift blame, you will never be free from errors. If you are not humble, to receive help will be difficult. This is deadly.

I have realized that what you call error may seem like a norm to another person; however, there are general errors that others agree with. Every profession has a mistake.

In the healthcare industry, charting the wrong dosage is an error that may cost you your license. While adding a few zeroes to a check or payment receipt may also cost you your job as a banker, but there are some basic life mistakes that you must learn to overlook.

I had a fine art assignment during high school, and in excitement to practice what I was taught in school, I decided to start the assignment on the school bus. Well, doing assignments on the school bus is not a bad idea; it is a great idea, but I failed to understand that not all kinds of assignments can be done on a bus. As I picked my brush and finished my drawing, someone splashed water on me, and my painting got soaked. It was a painful experience. I got home, started all over again, but I forgot to include borderlines to my drawing; hence I got a ridiculously low mark for the drawing.

If I had been scared of failure, two things would have happened to me:

- I would have developed a hatred for fine arts, which would have continuously made me fail arts

- I would never attempt my assignment because I would assume that I would fail.

Mistakes are bound to happen, and the sad reality is that some mistakes could take people's lives away, make people lose their jobs, family, or items, but the truth remains that even amid these mistakes, you can still make headway.

Sometimes, you make some decisions, and after a few months, you realize you made the biggest mistake of your life. Dear friend, you can bury the past. You should never allow your errors or mistakes to determine the result of your life. Whether you made mistakes in your life, family, work, or relationships, never lose hope.

These factors don't mean you won't tour the path of error, but it guides avoidable ones. Though the fact is avoidable and unavoidable errors will come our way, our response to it matters. Your response in humility and willpower to bruise the head of shame instead of burying yourself in the coffin of regret. I need you to know that it is a good thing to make mistakes; it should be noted that making mistakes is different from being careless or intentionally destructive after all you need to know has been said and done. I know you have been insulted for your slip-ups, mistakes, and violation of instructions; I want to tell you that those experiences are normal. It is normal for those who don't understand the magic in errors to lash at you with their tongue and sign you out of greatness with their words. But it is abnormal for you to succumb to their negative testimonies after all that you have read and heard. Make use of the magical quality in your error, which others never see, learn from it, and outgrow it no matter how hard it may be. Let people know: the rejected stone will become the chief cornerstone of many success stories. Soar!

Chapter 29: The Power to Decide and the Power Not To

Good decision making involves choosing the best actions and outcomes for yourself. Often. The inability to make decisions for oneself springs up from low-self-esteem, irresponsibility, and even lack of accountability. Possessing the power to decide is one drive you will need to achieve your dreams.

Your current state and level of achievement result from the past decisions you have made, and where you would be in a few years is also dependent on the strength of the choices you make now.

Being a Good Decision Maker

We could say that making apt decisions is a skill every purpose-driven individual must possess. Decision-making skills depict your competence in choosing between the options you have. This skill is acquired when you can process available information and speak with the right people.

It is paramount to understand these processes.

What Are Your Features and Personality Traits?

There are natural features about yourself that can help your decision making. Knowing yourself can help you determine how you make decisions and how to improve on them. Some of your traits and features that could influence the decisions you make are:

- **Risk:** Are you the kind of person who loves taking a risk? As good as this trait can be, it also has its hold on your decision; how? Risk-takers usually make decisions without taking out time to consider the consequences or the outcome. When you understand your inclinations, you would know when to go against your instincts and follow them.

- **Pride**: Another word for this could be termed as "overconfidence." It is a widespread phenomenon that influences your decision prowess. If you possess this trait, you would always tend to think too highly of yourself in terms of your knowledge, performance, and input overall. Asking for help when you are confused often helps you improve your skills and experience and even help you make better decisions.

- **Natural prejudice:** Factually, every individual has a hidden opinion, a natural preference, whether good or bad. For instance, have you ever made assumptions about

205

some people or situations? And then, you make decisions based on that. The things that interest you naturally have a way of coming in between your choices. So, before taking any step, think carefully if you are letting your natural concerns and prejudice get in the way of the decisions you make.

- **The goals you wish to achieve:** Every choice you make should align with the goals you want to achieve. When you have your goals, it will help and serve as a direction in making great choices. When you understand the results you want to see, making good choices becomes much easier. For instance, if you have two job offers, weighing your goals would give you a clearer vision of which jog you should go for.

- **Your past decisions:** As you make decisions, it gives you more experiences. What decisions have you made in the past? How were the results? How can you make better decisions from the mistakes you have made? As you make new decisions, reflect on the past, the good and bad ones, the approaches you used, etc. This would help you make better decisions.

- **Gather Information:** Why are you deciding the first place? What options do you have? What are the impacts of these options, and how advantageous are they to you and the people around you? Collecting enough (relevant) information would give you the confidence to act decisively.

- **Carefully weigh all the options you have:** Making decisions can be challenging, especially when there are many juicy options. However, the more options you consider, the more you increase your chances of making great decisions. Carefully examining them and talking to trusted people around you can give you more insight.

- **Take your time:** It is always better to take your time rather than making pressured decisions; the outcomes are rarely positive. When you make hasty decisions, they are usually surrounded by prejudice and your inclinations. Try to carve out more time, and this would help you reflect and make better options.

- **Embrace the results**: Whether you like it or not, every choice you make has an impact on those who are connected to you. Make a lot of considerations before going for your option; imagine the outcomes of your decisions.

- **Keep your mind open:** Often, you might have unconsciously made your choice already; you aren't sure. It is normal to conclude immediately, but don't act on it immediately; search for evidence, opinions, and then act on it. Stay open-minded until you have weighed all options.

- **Review your decision:** Think of your decision's outcomes. Would the purpose of the decision be achieved? If no, take your time to go over it again.

- **Take action:** Now you are good to go, take steps to your decision after considering all of the points above.

The Power of Your Decisions

Decisions go a long way. They speak the past, present, and even the future; that's how powerful they can be. In furtherance of this, let us see how your decisions' power goes a long way in your life.

- **They would keep you on track:** Setting your goals and plans is a decision on its own. Going ahead to weigh beneficial alternatives as you take steps is also a decision. You keep deciding on every level you attain. The power to decide helps you measure your goals and directs you on how well you can accomplish them.

- **Help you achieve goals:** The choices you make depend on how much you would achieve your goals. Making good decisions would help you overcome procrastination, laziness, unwillingness, and the list goes on.

- **Give you more experience:** Have you ever made a decision and you realized it wasn't favorable? If you come across such circumstances again, would you make the same mistake? Taking some decisions involves risk-taking. Over time, you would gain experiences and even be able to advise others on taking the right steps.

- **Self-confidence:** The ability to have an opinion of your own and even making it a reality via your decisions is a very bold step. Low confidence in one's self often springs up from the inability to take a stand. When you have the power to decide, it boosts your self-esteem, especially when you make correct choices.

- **Direction:** As aforementioned, having goals is a decision on its own. Your goals and decided to pursue them every day often will give you a clear vision.

In the conclusion of this chapter, your ability to make decisions is very paramount. It defines you, sets your standards, and determines how far you go in life. Even when you sit on the fence, you have still made a decision.

Chapter 30: Our Reputation – Our Idea of Ourselves Is Reflected on the Outside

I have standards, have my values, and do not engage in activities or engagements to soil my reputation. One of my core values is integrity, and I have a name to protect; hence, I will not do anything that will tamper with my name or my reputation.

The truth is our personalities reflect our ideas and values.

John is a Human Resource Manager for a banking firm, and he said one of the ways he interviews new employees and measures the credibility of their reputation. He said most times, and he asks them random questions such as, "What will you do if you find a sack that contains $1000 somewhere on your way to work?" he said many times he gets replies, "I will take it, and make use of it."

He said he also ask some other questions like, "Will you allow anyone to have sex with your partner for $10,000". He also said people gave them different answers, and many times he got the ideal employee by checking their answers.

Your reputation goes before you; it tells people about your values and your integrity.

Why a Good Reputation Is Important

It is clear and evident that a good reputation is vital in human lives. Today, many businesses and brands, and organizations triumph on the verge of having a good reputation. At the same time, the brands with a high societal reputation get more jobs than other brands with no reputation. Besides, a good reputation gives people credibility. Below are some benefits of having a good reputation:

- A good reputation makes you the best choice every day, every time. Have you ever tried to apply for a job where you have a lot of competitions? Have you ever struggled to have someone recommend you or refer you for a position? If you have struggled to achieve these at any time in your life, perhaps you should measure your reputation. What can society say about you? What can people say about your character and attitude?

- It makes people easily believe in you or trust you. I have had to recommend people for jobs and refer people, but I never recommend people I do not believe in. Whenever I believe in people, I find it easy to go the extra mile for them because I know they will represent me well in their various positions.

The Business of Good Reputation

Imagine that you can sell your reputation; how much would it be worth? Having a good reputation is a good business because it costs more than money. A good reputation helps you leverage freely on platforms of those who trust you or believe in you. You stand a chance of having recommendations for jobs, gigs, and contracts because of your reputation.

Moreover, if you intend to be a successful business owner, you need to invest heavily in your reputation.

How to Invest in Your Reputation

- Be actively involved in the community's service at your community level

- Volunteer for positions and responsibilities that will allow you to prove yourself to the world

- Be willing to network and connect with people

- Ask your family and friend to recommend you to someone who may need your service.

Your reputation is as important as your name; patiently invest in your reputation and achieve great results in your personal life.

Chapter 31: The Trap of Good People – Think First of Your Loved Ones and Then of Yourself

I once visited a mall, and I saw a little girl between the ages of 8 – 12 crying; I stopped and wondered why a girl so beautiful would have tears dripping down her cheeks with ice cream in her hands. At first, I thought she was crying because she did not want that ice cream flavor; well, everyone knows how dramatic some children can be. They just want to have what they want, and when their parent seems to turn a deaf ear to them, they cry the building down. I went close to her and squatted next to her; I asked her why she was crying with a big smile. She did not answer; I guess she pretended not to hear me, which I think is normal. *"Do you want another flavor or some extra wafers?"* I asked her again. She looked at me in the face. I could see innocence and purity in her eyes; I knew I had won her over, so I patted her and handed her one of the wafers in my bag.

"Why are you crying? Where is your mum?" I asked her

She looked at me again; this time around, she stared at me; I could hear her breathing heavily. So, I patted her shoulder again. *"I don't want, why are there so many children suffering?"* I listened to the tiny voice speak out some words, although she kept sniffing in between her words.

I tried to understand what she meant, so I asked her if she was alone or who brought her to the mall. She pointed at a slender woman who had been watching me so closely; I had seen how the woman stared at me effortlessly; I wonder if she was just interested in my good deeds, I never knew she was the mother of the poor child. The woman approached me and introduced herself.

"She is mad at me because I didn't donate to the UNICEF feed the child program." Her mother said. I tried to wrap my head around that. Why would she cry because her mum did not donate? Did she tell her mum to stay away from her? Was that why she did not want ice cream or wafers? All of these questions flooded my heart.

"I am not sure I understand you," I replied

"Well, Anny over here gets mad at me when I don't donate to help the poor. A few teenagers came over to meet me at the other stand and asked me to donate, but I had no money left, but Anny was angry at me. I have some money left, but it was for groceries and her snacks. Since then, she has been crying." Anny's mum summarized.

"Wow," I was speechless. I was surprised; Anny is just a young girl who is passionate about helping others. Her mum said she pays more attention to helping my friends and the needy around

her than having excess. I was delighted, and I picked interest in Anny. Anny has a kind heart, and her mum said she always wants to help others.

Being good to others should not be a feature of the age; you should never attribute goodness or kindness to children. Everyone should be good and act friendly towards others. I often mention the word goodness to people; they often say they are older now, and they don't have the luxury of time to act good to people. I am pleased to tell you that being good should be a norm; many people live in the world today who are in need, suffering, and even in great pain. But we must help them.

Why should you do good?

You should be good to people because you are good. When people ask why I am caring towards people, I tell them it is my person. The truth that I have discovered over time is that I have the strength to good towards people. I am not good at people because I want them to repay me with some kindness, but I am good because I can be good.

Many people take me for granted because I am too kind to them; what do I do?

Perhaps, that is the question in your mind right now. I know how hurtful it can be when people take your kindness for granted. I understand how Anny felt, and likewise her mum too. I had a long conversation with her mum, and her mum was concerned about her. Her mum thought she was too good; why would a young girl like her skip her meals, give out her money, prefer to starve herself to help others? But I told her mum, it is okay. They should let her be.

The Rule of Kindness

There is just one rule to kindness, do not do good because you want others to repay you. Moreover, you must ensure that you put your family and loved ones first. However, you need to be careful at this junction that you don't do what you don't like or feel under pressure to meet your loved ones' needs. I believe that you should have standards; to what extent can you meet your family's needs? These are the basic things that you will need to help others.

The Trap of Goodness

Are you surprised about this title? There is a trap called the goodness trap; this trap is often caused by the demands of different people around you. Many times, many people task people in their lives and depend on good people to meet their basic needs, which is entirely wrong. It is okay to ask some people to help you, but you must never depend on these people. Many people who trap good people in their lives do so because they are lazy and do not know that they depend on them or they are simply bad and do not care about the lives of others.

If your goodness has victimized you, you need to withdraw from such people and be wise in giving them. Being good is great; however, you must never give to people at the expense of your needs or your family's needs. It is wrong to help the needy with the money meant for your mortgage rent or school fees. There is time for everything, and you must understand the times and seasons in giving to people and doing good.

Chapter 32: The Importance of Your Physical and Mental Health; Only Then Can You Help Others

The World Health Organization is the body responsible for global health. They defined health as the state of complete physical, social, and mental well-being, not merely the absence of disease or infirmity in the person's life. Your mental health simply has to do with your psychological, emotional, and social well-being. WHO defines mental health as "mental well-being in which an individual realizes his or her abilities can cope with everyday stresses of life, can work productively and can make a contribution to his or her community. It guides the way you feel, think, and even act. Your mental health defines how you relate to other people, handle stress, and how you even make decisions. Your mental is very critical to every stage of life, from childhood to adulthood.

Many factors could serve as triggers to mental health problems such as experiences from life (trauma, abuse, violence, etc.), biological factors, infections, brain injury or defect, neurotransmitters, etc. when you are mentally stable; you would be able to realize your full capabilities, work fruitfully, manage life's stressors, be an addition to those around you and even the society at large.

Your physical health, on the other hand, has to do with your physical well-being. Physical wellness boosts adequate care of your body for perfect health and functioning. Many factors make up physical wellness, which should all be catered for without any being left out. In a nutshell, good physical health boosts the stability of physical activity, nutrition, and even mental well-being to make the body keep feeling at its peak.

When your mental health is poor, you stand the risk of chronic physical conditions, and when you have a chronic physical condition, you are at a high risk of exposure to poor mental health. Ways to boost your physical and mental health include; constant exercise and physical activity, intake of nutritious foods and a balanced diet, fostering social relationships, etc. all of these would help reduce factors that put your physical and mental health at risk.

Are Your Physical and Mental Health Related?

Studies have shown that when you engage your body in exercises, it boosts your mental health. When you were in school, you must have had this experience; your teacher was teaching in the class, and you and your colleagues seemed dull, and some were even sleepy already. Your teacher would then ask everyone to stand up and would involve all of you in some exercise. Do you recall that there is usually a sharp response in the classroom after the physical activities? This tells you that there is a direct link between your physical and mental health.

A good physical health practice like exercise also provides you with a better mental condition. For instance, when you exercise, it helps you mentally by easing you off trauma, depression, a sharper memory, better sleep, and even increases your level of self-esteem.

Also, depression often leads to heart and vascular diseases. Chronic ailments like heart diseases, cancer, and diabetes heighten the risk of depression.

Conclusively, when you are not fine in your body (physical), it affects your emotions, how you think, feel act, etc. (mental), and vice versa.

The Path to Physical and Mental Well-Being

One characteristic of every existing human is that; you have a goal to achieve, a purpose of fulfilling, a dream you wish to make come through, a professional area you want to major in, etc. when you do this, and you are solving one problem or the other. You are helping one person or the other. For instance, if you dream of becoming a nurse, it means you have a passion for healthy people day in and day out. However, there are so many life stressors that can put your plans in jeopardy. They are your Physical and Mental health.

It is paramount for your physical and mental stability to understand the correlation between your body's physical and mental health to keep fit in these two aforementioned areas. When you take practical steps to do these, you would understand how they are both connected. Your physical state directly links to how you feel mentally and how you even relate with people. To sustain a good physical state, you should do the following:

Physical activities are effective because they fight mental stressors like anxiety, fear, depression, trauma, etc.

Your physical and mental health influence the following; crime rate, educational outcome, development of good personal relationships, positive work input, drug abuse, and alcohol intake.

Things You Can Do for Your Physical and Mental Health

- **Set goals that are realistic:** What do you wish to achieve in all spheres of your life? Write them down and then draft out the steps and measures you need to achieve those goals. There is a great feeling that comes with achieved goals, and there is also a draining feeling that comes with unachieved goals. When your goals are realistic and you achieve them, it increases your self-esteem, thereby giving strength to your mental health.

- **Seek help when necessary:** some people have this funny notion of seeking help as a weakness sign. In contrast to this belief, seeking help is a sign of strength in every way. See a therapist from time to time, talk to trusted friends about what you are going through. These would go a long way.

- **Learn how to suck in stress:** Stress is one part of life that goal getters cannot avoid. It is left to you to build enough mental capacity to contain stress and keep moving.

- **Care for Your Body:** Engage yourself in physical activities every day for 30 minutes, give yourself a break when your body asks you for it, control your food intake and eat good food, take long walks, drink enough water, avoid alcohol and drug abuse, safe practice of sex, stay consistent with a 7-9 hour sleep every night, etc.

- **Stay around positive people:** Obvious observations and experiences have shown that individuals with strong social connections and family backgrounds are usually more affluent in health than those deficient in support. Mingle around with people who add value to your life, join social interest groups, and the likes.

- **You are priceless:** How you see yourself is dependent on how others would treat you. How others treat you has a direct impact on your behavior, whether you like it or not. So, give yourself enough love, attention, support, care, and kindness. Make time for yourself, learn new things, and engage in the things you love doing. I believe that the only person who can take care of you is you, and no one can do it better.

Your health status has a way of affecting those around you and the community at large. As an individual, you are entitled to taking care of people around you and other significant others in your life. There is a quota you have to contribute to society, an impact you would want to make. All of these cannot be achieved if you are not fit health-wise. Here three things good health can help you succeed:

- **Physical activities:** When you are active physically, it keeps your body in a top-notch condition. Evident parts of good physical health in your body include: strong bones, strengthened muscle, reduced risk of diseases like stroke, and an increase in energy level. An excellent physical health status keeps you active and enables you to carry out the activities you wish to

- **Nutrition:** A path to good nutrition of your body is eating a balanced diet, fruits, and vegetables. Constant checkup with your doctor is also valid. This would not only help prevent illness or diseases; it would also help your body to function at its peak.

- **Emotional stability:** Physical and mental well-being would help to improve your cognitive abilities and also help your learning skills, sharpen your thinking, and would also give you a good sense of self and the happenings around you.

In conclusion, when you are fit physically and mentally, you will find it easier to cope with stress, you find it easy to adapt to people at your place of work or even around you; you can understand why some people act the way to do, you can make excuses for people, you can forgive those who hurt you, you find it easy to counsel your friends, you find it easier to give a helping hand, certain activities and tasks become easier. Life becomes a better place for you.

Chapter 33: Living 100/100 - the Best Version of You

Have you ever looked at some people around you, and you wished you could talk the way they talk or handle issues the way they do? If yes, it shows that you know what you want, and you desire to be a great and successful person. But, the truth is many times, that is not the only reason you admire successful people. I have realized that most people easily admire and desire people, not because they desire to do the same things this individual does, but because they feel they do not have the other individual's strength.

Whenever I hear people say things like, "I wish I were just like her," "I wish I was as brilliant as her," "I wish my dad were Bill Gates or Barack Obama, I would be more successful," many people are living each moment of their lives with I wish, and certain dreams that may never come to pass. Is there any chance that elites such as Barack Obama and Bill Gates adopt grown-up children come to think of it? The highest they do for adults is to empower them and probably accept to be their godparents, but it is very rare for anyone to be willing to adopt adults as children. What does that tell you? Certain desires of yours will never come to reality, not because you are not hardworking, but because such desires can only exist in your imagination and fantasy. Wishing and clamoring to be the best friend of Donald Trump's child, or an acquaintance to Mark Zuckerberg, or the goddaughter to Brain Tracy is just a delusion; it wouldn't lead you anywhere. Why don't you pay attention to your growth? Why don't you desire to be that person that inspires others? I have realized that we can be the best version of ourselves only if we are willing to put more effort into our lives and activities.

Do you know that certain individuals also desire to do things the way you do? These individuals hold you in esteem and wish they could enjoy the same privilege you enjoy someday. That is just the irony of life; while you think you have no good in you, someone else sees the good, better, and best in you and admires it. As much as it is a great thing to bear in mind that certain people around you admire you, you must never forget that you are already living a good life, and you can live the best version of yourself. Living the best version of yourself is not all about how much money you have or how acquainted you are with the elites; it is all about realizing that you have all it takes to succeed in life.

Who are you? What can you do? What do you have? These are questions that you must have answers to if you want to succeed in life. The answers to these questions will help you live and achieve the best positions in life. Becoming the best version of yourself is not difficult and can be achieved easily; however, you have to be willing to implement some new things, be resilient, and never give up on your dream.

How to Live the Best Version of Yourself

Recognize That Being the Best Version of Yourself Should Be Your Goal and Not Anyone Else's

Imagine if Bill Gates's parents had wanted him to be a techie individual and a wealthy person. Yet, he had not been interested in majoring in Computer science and technology; instead, he wanted to become a singer. Do you think Bill Gates would be as famous and wealthy as he is today if he had lived his parents' dream? He could have achieved a few successes if he had lived his parents' dream; however, he would not be as fulfilled as he would be if he had been living his dream. You must make your dreams your priority; do not wait for anyone to make your dreams valid. Dear friend, your dreams are valid. Your dreams are true and can be achieved, so don't give up, no matter what happens.

Don't Be Afraid of Starting From the Beginning

One of the attitudes that I have always observed in people who still desire and wish to live their lives like others is that they are always afraid of starting. For instance, a young girl says she wants to be the first lady of America, and some other people may wish they are the children of Will Smith and many other wishes. The truth is these people are afraid of starting their lives. These successful men and elites had their fair share of failure, struggles, and some other tough times in life. These men did not suddenly accumulate wealth or got someone to dash them money; they worked for it. These people burned midnight candles, cried, lost money, and friendship. Let's take a look at Oprah Winfrey's life, and she is today one of the wealthiest and powerful women in the world; unfortunately, she was a victim of sexual abuse when she was a teenager. Today, thousands of young girls and women wish they had both the influence and wealth she had, but I have never heard anyone desire to pass through the struggles she faced in life.

Need I say this too, you can only get the best version of yourself when you become better than you used to be. What does that mean? The best version comes after improvement. While I can't outright condemn the act of wishing to be like everyone else, I must say that you should also work on yourself to get the best version you've ever imagined. The bottom line is to embrace the little beginnings and the journey so far.

Focus on Yourself, and Not Some Secrets

Who are you? What do you want? What is your biggest dream? What is your future ambition? The route to living your best life is to focus on yourself, ignore the side talks of mysteries and secrets. There is no specific secret to living your best life because you cannot use the same method or method. Living your best life can only happen when you discover yourself, so just pay attention to the abilities that you have and every innate capacity.

Be Truthful With Yourself

There is nothing more powerful than you being truthful with yourself.

"As I have said, the first thing is to be honest with yourself. You can never have an impact on society if you have not changed yourself. Great peacemakers are all people of integrity, of honesty, but humility." – Nelson Mandela

I love Nelson Mandela's quote on being truthful with oneself, and I realized that the great delusional state you can be in is to live in deception. Never lie to yourself. Whether you are lazy, hardworking, whether you are a liar, or you are a loyal person, you know who you are and what you do. Be truthful to yourself, do not lie to yourself about how you feel, stop living in denial. It is said that many people live in denial today; they struggle to accept their faults and weaknesses. Not accepting that you are weak or have certain flaws will not make you weaker or less human; instead, it makes you better.

Celebrate Your Small Wins

One of the habits I have learned to practice is the act of celebrating my small wins. I believe that no wins are too small to be celebrated, whether it is as small as selling my service for $5 or as big as winning a million-dollar contract. Celebrating your small wins helps you achieve your goals, instructs your mind to do better, and enables you to feel loved. Henceforth, make it a habit to celebrate your small wins, no matter how little they are.

Reflection Exercise

The essence of this exercise is to help you reflect on your life and how near you are to your goals.

- I encourage you to write five things you wish you could do better as an individual and write out the activities you can implement to make you better.
- Today, celebrate your wins and achievements from the beginning of the year and share it on your social media platforms.

Final Note

It is not enough to read a book without making efforts to take steps that can yield effective results. Now that you have completed this book, I believe that you have gained insight into habits and building habits. I also believe that you must have realized that no one gets successful in life by chance or luck; however, people achieve great success by practicing good habits, keeping a positive mind, and being disciplined.

Here are a few keynotes that you must never forget about habits, success, and your life as a whole:

- You are the first beneficiary of your habits, character, and its impacts.

- Eating healthy is more than just a habit; it is your responsibility to keep your body healthy. this means that starving your body of balanced meal is irresponsibility

- On the verge of changing the world, you may create enemies or have more friends, but you must never forget that the environment inherits a healthy environment.

- Always be a preacher of happiness. Happy people should also encourage others to be happy just the same way they are.

- You can create your habits, provided they are healthy and good.

- Friendship and relationships grow better when both parties in the relationship have good habits.

- Nobody gets worse, or dies from eating a balanced diet, except if the food is poisoned, but people die from malnutrition and poor dieting

- Learn to give back to the world; that is another way to create a world that never existed.

- Never be in a hurry to react to negative things quickly. Make it a habit to control your five sense organs, and see how much transformation you will experience.

- Your health is another source of wealth. Only a healthy body thinks appropriately.

- Never underestimate the power of you. You should believe in yourself. Never be timid to take the risk, and talk about yourself.

- There is something more valuable than money most times, and it is our integrity. You can make many millions when people recommend you; however, recommendations are only for people with a good reputation.

- Your reputation is gold; value it.

- There is power in your thought; always be positive about yourself and others around you.

- Commitments are like debt and wedding vows. Never make them if you know you will not be loyal to it.

- You can choose between good and evil, hatred and love, light and darkness, but always remember that not everyone has a mind of their own. Never pressure anyone into wrongdoings.

- Be the reason someone is happy and fulfilled.

- Be your motivation.